Edited by Ed Zotti
Published by Ballantine Books

THE STRAIGHT DOPE

MORE OF THE STRAIGHT DOPE

RETURN OF THE STRAIGHT DOPE*

*Forthcoming

KNOW

THE FUN STUFF YOU NEVER LEARNED IN SCHOOL

IT

ALL!

ED ZOTTI

BALLANTINE BOOKS • NEW YORK

To Ryan and Annie, who will soon be
pestering their father
with questions of their own.

Copyright © 1993 by Ed Zotti
Illustrations copyright © 1993 by Randy Verougstraete

All rights reserved under International and Pan-American Copyright
Conventions. Published in the United States by Ballantine Books, a
division of Random House, Inc., New York, and simultaneously in Canada by Random House of
Canada Limited, Toronto.

Library of Congress Catalog Card Number: 92-90078

ISBN: 0-345-36232-2

Text design: Michaelis/Carpelis Design Associates

Manufactured in the United States of America
First Edition: July 1993
10 9 8 7 6 5 4

CONTENTS

KNOW
IT
ALL!

INTRODUCTION

I went through sixteen years of education, just like everybody else. And just like everybody else, I kept asking myself the same thing the whole time: When do we get to the stuff I want to know about, as opposed to what somebody else *thinks* I should know? We never did, even in college. School left me with a lot of unanswered questions.

Finding out the answers to those questions has been my mission in life ever since. I edit a column called "The Straight Dope" that appears in weekly papers around the country. The idea behind "The Straight Dope" is simple: You ask the questions, we find out the answers. We pick up where most people's educations left off.

The author of the column is the mysterious Cecil Adams, the World's Smartest Human Being. Cecil knows everything, and he's never wrong. You've probably met people like this. The difference is, Cecil really *does* know everything.

Of course, Cecil and I don't answer just *any* question in "The Straight Dope." We skip the fan magazine, "where-can-I-write-to-Madonna" stuff. We don't give advice on how to get along with your mother-in-law or how to get the stains out of your carpet.

The questions we get psyched about are the ones that have always bugged people. Questions like:

• If you were in an elevator and the cables snapped,

could you save yourself by jumping up at the last second?

• Why do your toes and fingers wrinkle in the bathtub?

• Where are all the baby pigeons?

• How do the astronauts go to the bathroom in space? (Don't tell me you haven't wondered.)

Cecil and I published two collections of columns, *The Straight Dope* and *More of the Straight Dope*. They've been quite popular, and soon we plan to publish a third collection called *Return of the Straight Dope*. We hope you'll get a chance to read—okay, to *buy*—these books someday.

But it occurred to us there was a problem with them. We assumed you knew an awful lot to start with—that you had a college education, basically. If you weren't quite that far along yet, a lot of the *Straight Dope* would be over your head.

So we wrote this book. Actually, *I* wrote it. I figured what the heck, I was qualified. Maybe I wasn't the World's Smartest Human Being, but having worked with Cecil all these years, I was one Pretty Darn Smart Guy.[1]

The main difference between the *Straight Dope* books and this one is that here I explain things a little more. Look, *I* know what the schools are like these days. You're lucky if you come out knowing how to write your name. So in this book I fill in the missing details.

But let's get one thing straight. I'm not trying to write an *educational* book here. Educational books are the kind your parents buy you. They figure if you read them you'll turn out to be a child genius, get into Harvard, and win the Nobel Prize. Nothing like a little pressure, right?

---

[1]Also, to be honest, they gave me a Real Big Advance.

Well, relax. I don't care if you get into Harvard or not. All I'm trying to do is pass along a little information—information that you'll need to survive.

And boy, do you ever need it. If there's one thing Cecil and I have learned over the years, it's this: *80 percent of everything you hear is wrong.*

For instance, you may have heard that water goes down the drain counterclockwise in the Northern Hemisphere and clockwise in the Southern Hemisphere, due to the rotation of the earth. Well, guess what: it doesn't.[2] You'll be surprised to find out in the pages ahead how much of what you've heard really isn't so. In this book we deal strictly with the facts. Believe me, the truth is weird enough.

Now, you may say, what difference does it make which way the water goes down? Right off the bat, not much. But the way I see it, if you start buying the business about drains, next thing you know you'll be believing politicians and used-car salesmen. Think of this book as training for life.

One more thing. Just because this book is aimed at (ahem) young people, don't figure I'm going to use nothing but short words and have it come out sounding like baby talk. If I feel I need a big word, I damn well intend to use one.

Technical words are in **boldface,** like so. Usually I'll try to define them as they come up and tell you how to pronounce them. Other big words I'll put in just to break up the monotony, and these I won't define. If you don't know what they mean, you've got two choices: Ask somebody

[2]Usually. If you want to know more, you'll just have to read the book.

or go look it up. Too much trouble? Deal with it.

We've tried to cover the basic questions of existence in this book. If there's anything we've left out—and there's always something—just ask. Send your questions to:

Ed Zotti
c/o Ballantine Books
201 E. 50th St.
New York, NY 10022

ANIMALS

HOW DO HOUSEFLIES MANAGE TO LAND ON THE CEILING UPSIDE DOWN?

Maybe you never wondered about things like this. But *I* did, which is how I got to be such a Darn Smart Guy.

Think about it. When the fly is heading toward the ceiling, it's flying right side up. When it lands on the ceiling, it's upside down. Obviously at some point along the line it does a flip. But when? And where? And how?

For a long time the most popular theory was that the flies did a "barrel roll" right before landing—that is, a quick flip to the side. (See illustration.)

But it wasn't until high-speed cameras were developed that scientists could find out for sure. These cameras took so many pictures per second that at least one of them was bound to show the fly doing its flip.

Old (wrong) theory of how flies land on the ceiling: the barrel roll.

Surprisingly, the scientists found the fly didn't do a barrel roll; instead, it did a back flip like a trapeze artist. As the fly neared the ceiling, it stuck its forward legs over its head. As soon as it touched down (or touched up, I suppose we should say), it swung the rest of its body up until all six feet were firmly planted on the ceiling. (The fly *stays* planted on the ceiling, of course, because it has sticky pads on the bottoms of its feet.)

How flies really *land on the ceiling: back flip.*

How does the fly get *off* the ceiling? I have no idea. I figure I should leave *some*thing for the coming generation to find out.

Do insects sleep? Do they dream?

Let's put it this way. They get quiet and curl up and look like they're sleeping. But what's really going on inside those molecule-sized brains nobody knows.

The one sure way to know if an animal is sleeping is to hook it up to a machine that measures electrical patterns in the brain. That's how we know that birds and mammals—animals like dogs, cats, cows, and pigs—actually sleep.

The problem with bugs is they don't have enough brains to hook the wires to. (This is a common problem in our society.) So we don't really know what they're doing.

The same goes for dreaming. In humans, dreams often occur during what's called "rapid eye movement" sleep— REM sleep for short. Rapid eye movement means your eyes dart around under your closed lids. REM sleep occurs for several hours a night in most humans.

As with brain waves, though, you need a special machine to detect REM sleep. We know it occurs in cats and dogs, and some people take that as a sign that cats and dogs dream. But insects are too small to hook the machine up to.

The general feeling among scientists is that bug brains are so crude insects barely *think,* much less dream. The bugs aren't saying, so we'll just have to leave it at that.

Is it true cats can suck the breath from babies?

Not literally. But there is a chance a cat can harm a sleeping infant, so some cat experts say you shouldn't leave a cat and a baby alone together.

It's not that cats have it in for kids. They just like to sleep in warm places. One guaranteed warm place is a sleeping human. Every once in a while a cat owner wakes up to find a small furry being stretched out on his chest or sometimes even his face.

That's no big deal for an adult, but for a kid it's a different story. If a cat decided to relax on a snoozing baby, the baby might suffocate. Or so they say. I'll admit I haven't been able to dig up any cases where this actually occurred, but who wants to be the first? Keep those cats in the kitchen where they belong.

CAN CATS SEE IN COLOR?

I know what you're thinking. How can they *tell* if cats can see in color? Cats can't *talk*.

Come on, you think scientists are dummies? One way they test these things is by figuring out ways to link color to food.

For instance, suppose you were trying to find out if a cat could tell the difference between green and gray. You set up two doors. Behind the green door you put a tasty heap of fish. Behind the gray door you put nothing.

If the cat can see color, eventually he'll learn he's always supposed to open the green door if he wants to eat. But if he's color-blind, he'll never learn. He'll push the gray door open half the time and the green door the other half.

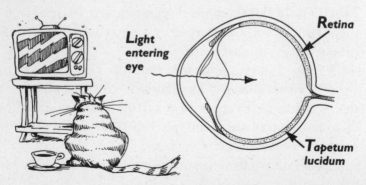

Light entering eye

Retina

Tapetum lucidum

Using methods like this, scientists many years ago decided that cats were color-blind. The cats never seemed to figure out which door they had to push to get the food.

But other scientists were suspicious. They looked at the **retina** (REH-tih-nuh) inside a cat's eye. The retina takes light entering the eye and converts it into electrical signals that are then sent to the brain. (See illustration.)

The retina is made up of thousands of tiny nerve cells. In humans, some of the cells are cone shaped, and others are rod shaped. It's believed the cones detect color during daylight, while the rods detect light and shadow (that is, black and white) at night.

The thing is, cats have cones in their retinas just like us. Knowing this, some scientists thought cats might be able to see color if they really tried.

So they retested the cats with fish. After about 10 million tries, the cats finally got the hang of it. The scientists concluded that cats were physically able to see color, they just were real slow learners.

That's probably because cats in the wild hunt mostly at night, when color vision is of no use to them. For a cat, learning to use color vision is like learning to knit with your feet. You could do it, but why would you want to? Cats obviously feel the same way.

WHY DO A CAT'S EYES GLOW IN THE DARK?

It's pretty spooky, all right. You come across a cat in a dark room, and when it looks up at you its eyes have this weird greenish-yellow glow. The glow is called "eye shine," and it's one of the reasons cats in ancient times were believed to have supernatural powers.

Actually, eye shine occurs in a lot of animals, not just cats. If you have ever been driving in the country at night and seen a deer's eyes caught in the headlights, you've probably noticed the same spooky glow. You also see it in dogs.

Eye shine is caused by a part of the animal's eye called the **tapetum lucidum** (tuh-PEET-um LOO-sih-dum). It's a special layer behind the retina that acts like a mirror. Light strikes the retina, passes through it, bounces off the tapetum lucidum, and passes through the retina again. This gives the animal two chances to see something. That's important at night, when there isn't much light and you have to make the best use of what little there is. The tapetum lucidum is especially important for cats, which prowl about a lot at night.

Why do you just see eye shine at night, rather than all the time? Because of something called **pupil dilation** (PYOO-pull die-LAY-shun). The pupil is the black spot in the center of the eye. It's surrounded by the **iris,** the part of the eye that has color, such as blue or brown.

The iris **dilates** (adjusts) to control the amount of light passing through the pupil into the eye. When the iris is wide open and the pupil is as large as it can be, we say the eye is fully dilated.

A cat's (or anybody's) pupils dilate when it's dark to allow the most possible light into the eye. They also dilate whenever something new comes along (like you) that the cat wants to get a good look at. The more the pupil dilates, the more of the tapetum lucidum is visible, and the more eye shine you see. Of course, it also helps if there's something bright to reflect off the tapetum lucidum, such as car headlights or a flashlight.

It's all perfectly logical and normal. But I don't mind telling you it still gives me the creeps.

Is it true horses sleep standing up?

You've probably seen those westerns where the bad guys sneak up on the good guys' camp at night and steal the horses. The horses are always just standing there, ready at a moment's notice to be stolen or stampeded or whatever it is the bad guys have in mind.

"What's the deal?" you ask. "Don't horses ever lie down?" Actually, they do—sometimes. When they're sick, for instance. Or when a mare is giving birth (or "foaling," as they say).

But not usually. Horses can go for days and sometimes even weeks without ever leaving their feet. They have the ability to lock their knees into a standing position and sleep at the same time. If you tried the same thing, you'd fall over and brain yourself. Not horses.

Some experts say horses are more comfortable and use less energy when standing. Part of the problem with lying down is that the great weight of the horse's body can make it difficult to breathe.

Horses aren't the only critters who sleep standing up. So do flamingoes. What's more, they do it on one leg, with the other leg tucked beneath them, while standing in shallow water. Why? Mainly to impress the tourists is my guess, but being in the water also makes it pretty hard to sneak up on a sleeping flamingo.

Is it true that one dog year equals seven human years?

Not exactly. Several improved formulas have been suggested. Here's one of the simpler ones:

First dog year = 21 human years
Each later dog year = 4 human years

If you've got a 7-year-old dog, it's 21 + (6 x 4) = 45 in human years. In the prime of life, in other words. A 10-year-old dog is 57 in human years, and a 15-year-old dog is 77.

That makes a lot more sense than the old 7-to-1 rule, which would make a 15-year-old dog 105—in other words, unbelievably ancient. Saying the dog is the equivalent of 77 is a lot more reasonable.

Where are all the baby pigeons?

Everybody asks this question. It's never baby squirrels or baby sparrows or baby ants, just baby pigeons. I don't get it.

Not that there's any big mystery. Pigeons build nests just like other birds. But they don't put them in trees if they can avoid it. Pigeons originally came from North Africa, where they built their nests on cliff ledges so they could stay out of sight of their enemies on the ground.

In cities, where many pigeons live, the nearest thing they can find to a cliff ledge is a ledge or windowsill on the side of a tall building. Another place they like to hide their young is the ironwork under bridges—anywhere that's out of sight. Scout around in a few such locations and chances are you'll turn up a pigeon nest or two.

Okay, so where are all the dead pigeons?

This is another question I hear a lot. The answer is pretty much the same as for baby pigeons. When pigeons get old and sick, they go to someplace out of sight where their enemies can't find them. A lot of times that's where they die.

In fact, not far from the office where I work, there's a pigeon graveyard. Humans think it's just an overpass, but dozens of pigeons young and old hang out in the ironwork underneath. Most days you can usually find the bodies of a couple of pigeons who've passed on to the Great Park Statue in the Sky. Scavengers—rats, usually—quickly drag off what's left. Very sad, but it beats having the poor little guys pile up in the streets.

How come birds perching on electric wires aren't electrocuted?

Because they're not **grounded.** Because they don't **complete a circuit.** Because they don't create a **short.** These are all ways of saying the same thing.

Without getting into the technical details, we can say that what an electric current wants most in life is to get from one side of the electrical generator to the other. Usually the only way to do this is by moving through the "hot" wire to the light bulb or toaster or whatever, doing some work (i.e., lighting the light, toasting the toast, etc.), and then returning by way of the "neutral" wire to the other side of the generator.

Once in a while, however, someone or something offers the electricity a shorter and easier path back home. If you're standing in a puddle and you touch a live wire, the current will jump from the wire to your body to the puddle. From there it will return to the generator by way of the ground. You'll receive a shock and perhaps even be killed, all because you were *grounded*—that is, because your body created a *short circuit*.

But birds aren't grounded. They don't offer the current a shorter route home. So they can perch on an electric wire all day and night. But don't envy them. At least you get to sleep indoors.

Is it true chickens can run around with their heads cut off?

As a matter of fact, it is. I've actually seen a photo of a headless chicken. It was in the October 22, 1945 issue of *Life* magazine.

It seems a farmer named L. A. Olsen wanted to kill a chicken for dinner one day. Old Mike (that was the chicken's name) got elected, and the farmer got out his ax.

Trouble was, the farmer's aim wasn't too good, and he didn't chop all of Mike's head off—just the top three-fourths. The **brain stem**—the part of your brain that keeps your heart and lungs and such working—is located in the bottom fourth.

So Mike didn't die. He just sort of waddled off and

hung out with the rest of the chickens. The farmer, seeing the hand of fate in this and figuring he might get struck by a bolt of lightning if he tried to zap Mike again, decided to leave well enough alone. He actually fed Mike for several weeks with an eyedropper, and stuffed some corn down his throat, too.

What finally became of Mike we do not know. But the rumor that he grew up to be vice president of the United States is totally untrue.

Is it true that, according to the laws of aerodynamics,[1] it's impossible for bumble-bees to fly?

It's time to put this silly story to rest. Obviously they do fly, and there's nothing in the laws of aerodynamics that says they can't. But it's easy to see where the idea got started. Compared to its body, a bumblebee's wings are pretty small. An airplane built like that would never get off the ground.

But bumblebees aren't like airplanes, they're like helicopters. The blades on a helicopter aren't very big either, but they do manage to get the helicopter into the air.

The difference between an airplane wing and a helicopter blade is that a helicopter blade moves through the air much faster. The higher the speed, the more the lift that is created.

A bumblebee's wings move, too—hundreds of times per second. They don't move in quite the same way that a

[1]That's air-oh-die-NAM-iks, in case you were wondering. Aerodynamics is the science of flight through the air, as opposed to space.

helicopter's blades move (they flap, rather than spin), but they create enough lift to get the bumblebee flying.

IS IT TRUE THAT IF RABBITS COULDN'T CHEW ON THINGS, THEIR TEETH WOULD GROW SO LONG THEY COULDN'T EAT AND THEY'D DIE?

Amazing but true. In humans and most other critters the teeth grow to a certain length and then stop. Not so with rabbits. Their teeth grow all the time. The only thing that keeps them from looking like bunny vampires is that their teeth rub against each other when they chew. This wears the teeth down to a normal length.

But sometimes rabbits get a bad case of **underbite**—reverse buck teeth. Their teeth don't line up right, so they don't wear away and instead grow to unbelievable lengths. Since this prevents the rabbit from chewing, chances are it will starve unless someone—preferably a veterinarian—comes along and trims its teeth.

IS IT TRUE ELEPHANTS NEVER FORGET?

Yup. We know this because of an experiment many years ago by a professor in Germany. He taught an elephant to choose between two wooden boxes, one marked with a square, the other with a circle. The box with a square had food in it, the other didn't.

This elephant was no Einstein. It took 330 tries before it figured out that "square" meant "food." Once it got the idea, though, things went a lot quicker. Soon the professor could put any two markings on the boxes. The elephant would experiment a few times, figure out which sign meant "food," then pick the right box from there on out.

Big deal, you say. Ah, but there's more. The professor came back a year later and tested the elephant again using the old markings—circles, squares, and so on. Amazingly enough, the elephant *still remembered* which markings were the signs for food. Heck, after a year, *I* wouldn't remember.

That's why elephants are so popular in circuses. It may take them a while to learn the act, but once they've got it, they've got it for good. If only all performers were as reliable.

Is it true turkeys are so stupid they'll look up at the sky when it rains and drown?

Turkeys are dumb, but they're not *that* dumb. Farmers think they are, though. In fact, I've had farmers swear the drowning-turkey story is true. But when I say, "Listen, you mean to tell me you actually stood out there in the rain and watched those poor birds die?" they admit they didn't. They came out afterward, found a few dead gobblers, and jumped to conclusions.

The trouble with turkeys is that when they're very young (up to eight or nine weeks) they have down instead of feathers. The down doesn't hold their body heat in very well, and it's easy for them to become badly chilled if the weather turns cool. If they get caught in a sudden rainstorm, they can get so cold they die. It's sad. Instead of making fun of the turkeys, we should be buying them raincoats and galoshes.

Do fish sweat?

Not in the usual sense. The idea behind sweating is that water collects on your skin, and when the wind comes along it turns the water to vapor and carries it away. The vapor takes with it some of the heat from your body. Result: You cool off. But since there's no wind underwater, it wouldn't do fish any good to sweat. So they don't.

Some fish do something like sweating, though. When we sweat, in addition to water we lose salt. Saltwater fish have to unload a lot of salt, too, because they pick up so much from the water around them. Special "salt cells" help them to do this. The cells are near the fish's skin and put salt the fish doesn't need back in the water. So saltwater fish *sort* of sweat. But for the real thing you need land animals.

Is it true that one of the major threats to the world environment is . . . cow burps?

Aw, you've been reading ahead. Believe it or not, some scientists think cow burps are a major menace to life on earth.

•

Cow burps contain a gas with no smell or color called **methane** (MEH-thayn). Methane is basically the same stuff that's used in gas stoves. In other words, it can burn. Cows burp up between 200 and 400 quarts of this stuff *per day*, or 50 million tons per year. No kidding.

Scientists are concerned about what happens when the methane gas that the cows burp floats up into the atmosphere. Methane, you see, adds to the **greenhouse effect.**

Probably you have heard of the greenhouse effect. Some scientists fear that chemicals in the atmosphere are trapping heat that would normally escape into outer space, much as the glass walls of a greenhouse trap heat inside. As a result, the earth is becoming warmer. If it becomes too warm, crops may fail and the polar ice caps may melt, causing flooding. It'll be so hot in the summer you won't be able to go outside.

Methane isn't the only thing causing the greenhouse effect. The **carbon dioxide** (die-AHK-side) produced by cars and factories (and by us, for that matter) plays an even bigger part. But methane is right up there.

Why do cows burp up so much methane? Mainly because of their eating habits. Cows aren't out there eating mashed potatoes and gravy. They eat hay and grass.

Hay and grass aren't easy to digest. In fact, the only way cows manage it is that (1) they chew their food a very long time, and (2) they have tiny creatures called **bacteria** in their innards that help break down hay and grass into something a cow's body can use.

But the bacteria do a pretty sloppy job. What they don't take care of the cows burp up as methane.

Your next question probably is: Why are we suddenly

blaming cows? There have *always* been cows.

True. As a matter of fact, cows aren't the only source of methane in the atmosphere. You can also blame rice paddies, swamps, oil drilling, the burning of the Amazon rain forest, even (don't laugh) termites. (One researcher thinks termites make even more methane than cows— 150 million tons a year.)

But let's face it, there's not much you can do about termites. Cows make a much bigger (and therefore easier) target. Besides, there are more cows now than there used to be—1.2 billion, by one count. That's a lot of burps.

So what do we do, give the cows Pepto-Bismol? Might not be such a bad idea. One scientist thinks if we fed the cows special drugs, they'd make less methane. But it's not very clear how you'd do this for 1.2 billion cows.

That leaves only one solution. Panic. Call me if you come up with any better ideas.

Do Goats Really Eat Tin Cans?

No, but you can see where the idea got started. While goats don't *eat* tin cans, they do *chew* on them—not because they like the metal, but because they want the glue that holds the labels on.

We can't digest glue, but goats are different. They have special bacteria in their guts, just like cows do. The bacteria help them break down the glue.

Glue is often made from animal or plant products, so it has some food value—but not much. Chew on enough cans, though, and you can get by. If you're a goat, I guess you can't be too fussy.

WERE THERE EVER REALLY SUCH THINGS AS FLEA CIRCUSES?

You better believe it. Obviously, before the invention of color TV, people were pretty desperate for entertainment.

Why don't we see flea circuses anymore? Partly because there's a lack of top-quality flea talent.

Fleas live on blood, and human blood gives them the most get-up-and-go. Years ago, when people weren't as fussy about cleanliness as they are today, human-fed fleas were pretty easy to come by. Today most fleas are found on dogs. Dog-fed fleas lack the same drive and ambition.

What did the fleas in a flea circus *do*? Lots. You could have flea orchestras playing flea music. (Not the best music, maybe, but what do you want, Beethoven?) Boy fleas could pull girl fleas (I admit it's a little hard to tell them apart) in little wagons. They could dance and play cards—I could go on and on.

A flea circus wasn't something you could stage in the Hollywood Bowl. It's not that you couldn't fill the seats; it's just that nobody could see the performers if they were more than a few feet away. A typical flea theater consisted of a small table for a stage surrounded by several chairs.

To make up for the lack of seating, flea circus owners staged as many as six shows an hour. Incomewise it wasn't up there with a Bruce Springsteen concert, but you didn't have to split the take with the performers, either.

WHY DO EARTHWORMS CRAWL ON THE SIDE-WALK AFTER IT RAINS?

Earthworms breathe air, just like you and me. When it rains, their holes fill with water. If they didn't get out of the house (and onto the sidewalk), they would drown. Take pity on a flood victim and watch where you step.

WHAT'S THE DIFFERENCE BETWEEN ALLIGATORS AND CROCODILES?

Not much—but they're not the same animal, as some people think. They're more like cousins.

Alligators are more common. In the United States they can be found in swamps and along rivers throughout the South. Crocodiles live only in southern Florida.

Alligators are said to have a sweeter temper than crocodiles. (Sweeter, not sweet. The sweetest tempered alligator on earth is not a creature I would care to meet in a dark alley.)

Alligators and crocodiles look a lot alike, but there are differences. Alligators have wide snouts and usually their teeth don't show when their mouths are closed. Crocodiles have narrow snouts and scary-looking fangs that stick out from their lower jaws. If you've got some big lizard after you, I suppose noticing these details may not be high on your list of priorities. But don't worry: we'll be able to tell what it was from the bite marks.

WHY DO FLIES SWARM AROUND A FIXED SPOT IN THE AIR?

It depends. If there's nothing obvious around to attract the flies' interest, then usually the big draw is the other flies.

They're mating, you see. Swarming flies (often they're called gnats) don't live very long and they have to make hay while the sun shines, so to speak. We won't go into the details. Let's just say that years from now you'll probably spend some time in bars that operate along similar lines.

WHY DO GEESE FLY IN A V?

Lots of guesses, no definite answers. Here are some of the top theories.

1. *The geese fly in a V to save energy.* Some people think each goose flies close to the one in front of it because the goose in front blocks the wind. With less wind resistance to overcome, the goose behind doesn't have to work as hard. (Race car drivers do something similar: they try to drive close to the car in front so they'll use less gas.)

Trouble is, for this idea to work, each goose would have to fly at a certain angle to the one in front and maintain a certain distance in between. And they'd all have to flap their wings at the same time. But they don't. The birds wander all over the place and flap their wings any which way.

2. *It helps the geese stay together.* The idea here is that by

keeping the bird in front of them in view, the geese won't get lost. Geese have easy-to-spot tail markings that make this easier. Doubters, however, claim that the geese's *honking* is what keeps them together. What's more, geese stay in formation after dark, when they can't see the goose in front of them.

3. *The geese fly in a* V *so other geese can recognize them at a distance.* Why it's more important that one bunch of geese be able to recognize another bunch of geese I don't know, but that's the theory.

So there you have it—another muddle. Maybe some hotshot young scientist of the future can get this straightened out.

Do cats have belly buttons?

Sure. They just don't look like human belly buttons. Cat belly buttons are a long scar, often covered with hair, located just under the cat's rib cage. Almost all mammals have belly buttons because they all had, at one point, **umbilical** (um-BILL-i-kull) **cords.** Umbilical cords provide food and so on while the baby is still inside its mother's womb.

The exceptions are the **duckbill platypus** (PLAT-ee-puss), the **echidna** (eh-KID-nuh, also known as the spiny anteater), and Adam and Eve. The platypus and the echidna, which live in Australia, are born in eggs, so they don't have umbilical cords. As for Adam and Eve—well, think about it.

THE 2 BODY

CAN YOU DIE FROM PICKING YOUR NOSE?

You sure can. If you're the type who can't resist temptation, you might want to think about mittens.

To be sure, killing yourself by picking your nose wouldn't be easy. But suppose you were in there one day, digging away, when you put a bit too much muscle into it and broke the skin. And suppose further that your fingers were crawling with deadly germs. What next?

If today was not your day, a repulsive infection might take root in your nose. Repulsive infections in them-

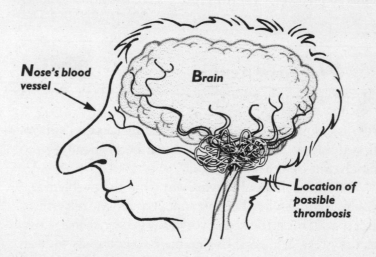

Nose's blood vessel

Brain

Location of possible thrombosis

selves aren't so bad. Someday, in fact, you may find yourself dating one. The problem would come if your infection spread downstream by way of your blood vessels.

The vein that carries blood out of your nose drains toward the back of your head. There it joins a lot of other veins, including the ones that drain blood out of your brain. (See illustration.)

If the infection in your nose reached the spot where all the veins join, it might create a blockage that would prevent blood from draining out of your head. This is a condition known as **intracranial thrombophlebitis** (in-tra-CRAY-nee-ull throm-bow-fleh-BITE-iss). As I understand it, your head basically would fill up like a water balloon.

I have never actually seen what happens next, so I'm not sure, for instance, that your head actually would explode. It would be a sight to see, though, so if you're a hard-core nose-picker and you notice the early warning signs (high fever, twitching, etc.), give the doc a call.

WHY DO WE ITCH?

It's disappointing to tell you this, but doctors don't know. If you ask me, certain people have been spending too much time on the golf course.

Doctors can usually figure out what the problem is if you're itching a lot. For instance, you might have fleas. But spot itching, the kind everybody gets once in a while, is a mystery. Someone did manage to come up with an impressive name for it, though: **punctate pruritus** (PUNK-tate proo-RIGHT-iss).[1]

Researchers aren't even sure *how* your body itches. They know it has something to do with the many tiny nerve endings in your skin. They also know it has something to do with the sense of pain, because people who can't feel pain anymore stop itching. At any rate, spot itching is harmless.

WHY DO YOUR FINGERS AND TOES WRINKLE IN THE BATHTUB?

The tips of your fingers and the soles of your feet are covered by a thick, tough layer of skin called the **stratum corneum** (STRAH-tum KOR-nee-um). (Stratum corneum is Latin for "horny layer," but this is something I would just as soon not mention to a bunch of teenagers.)

When this layer of skin soaks for a long time, it absorbs water and expands. Trouble is, on your fingers

---

[1] You may not think this sounds like progress, but that's because you haven't been to medical school yet. There you will learn the usefulness of the **proper terminology** ("big words"). For example:

PATIENT: Doctor, I've got an itch on my elbow that's driving me nuts.
YOU (looking thoughtful): Hmm. Sounds like a case of **punctate pruritus**. We'll have to amputate. Nurse, hand me that chain saw.
NURSE: Chain saw, check.
CHAIN SAW: BRRRR-UPPPPP!
PATIENT (perspiring heavily): Uh, doctor, isn't there some alternative?
YOU: Of course, there's always **psychoanalysis** ("seeing a shrink"). You come in here every week for the next 20 years and pay me 90 bucks an hour to listen to you complain about how your mother never loved you. You'll still have the itch, but at least you'll know *why*.
PATIENT (pulling out checkbook): Now we're talking. When do we start?

You get the picture.

and toes there's no place for it to expand *to*. So it just buckles, like asphalt roads do sometimes in the summer sun. (See illustration.)

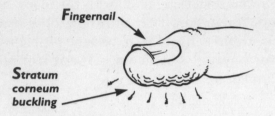

WHAT HAPPENS WHEN YOU CRACK YOUR KNUCKLES?

Everyone for 10 feet around gets grossed out of existence, that's what happens. What physically happens once you start tugging is that bubbles form in the sac of liquid that surrounds your knuckles. Keep it up and the bubbles pop—and that's what you hear. Some say knuckle-crackers are more likely to get arthritis later in life, although this has never been proven. But it would serve them right.

IS IT POSSIBLE TO BE TICKLED TO DEATH?

Hard to believe, but the answer may be yes.[2] At any rate, it's possible to die laughing. We know this because every once in a while people are struck by mass laughing fits and some of them *do* die. No kidding.

[2]Don't get any ideas.

The last case of mass laughing fits I've heard of affected about a thousand people in the African country of Tanganyika (now Tanzania) in 1963. They couldn't stop laughing for several days.

Most of the people involved in a mass laughing fit get better, but a few don't. You can't eat or sleep while you're laughing, so there's a chance you could die of a combination of starvation and exhaustion.

But could you be *tickled* to death? Maybe. It's said the ancient Romans once used tickling to torture people to death. They'd strap some poor guy down and dip his feet in salt water. Then they'd bring a goat over to lick his feet. (Goats like salt.) The victim would laugh his head off—but meanwhile, the goat's rough tongue would be scraping the skin off his feet.

When the goat got done, they'd dip the victim's feet in salt water again and start over. Eventually the guy would die horribly, laughing all the while. So take it easy next time you're tickling your little sister.

WHY DO YOUR ARMS AND LEGS FALL ASLEEP SOMETIMES?

Sometimes it's because all the rest of you falls asleep. The problem arises when your arm or leg falls asleep and the rest of you doesn't. The affected part feels like a stick of salami—it's a dead weight with no sensation.

If your leg falls asleep and you try to walk on it, you could fall and hurt yourself. Even if you don't move, you may feel a sharp pain as the sleeping limb "wakes up."

Your arm or leg can fall asleep when a nerve gets pinched. At certain places in your body, such as your elbow, the nerves run close to the surface. If you press on one of those places for a long time (say, when you're leaning on your elbow trying to hold your head up during some fascinating discussion in school), nerve impulses can't get back and forth to your brain. Your arm then feels like it belongs to someone else.

Usually feeling returns within a few minutes after you shift your arm or leg to a new position. But if you pinch the same nerve again and again, sometimes it stays pinched. For example, people who work at desks with sharp edges sometimes lose feeling in parts of their hands because the edges press against the bottoms of their arms all day. Feeling may not return for days or even weeks. The solution is to get a different job. Or at least a desk with rounded edges.

WHAT ARE THOSE LITTLE SQUIGGLES YOU SEE FLOATING ON YOUR EYES WHEN YOU LOOK AT THE SKY?

They're called "floaters." An old name for them is "fluttering flies." To some people they look like spots; to others, like tiny threads. They're not on your eyes, though; they're *in* your eyes. That's why blinking doesn't make them go away.

Floaters are all that's left of the **hyaloid** (HI-uh-loyd) **artery**. The hyaloid artery carried blood to your eye and helped it grow before you were born, when you were still inside your mother's womb.

When your eyes were finished growing, the hyaloid artery withered and broke into pieces. But since these pieces were sealed up inside your eye, they had no place to go. You'll see them floating around the rest of your life, so you might as well get used to them.

Sometimes you may see a different kind of spot. These spots may look like tiny flickers of light or swarms of fireflies. Usually they last only a second or two. You may see them after receiving a blow to the head, or after doing a somersault or making some other sharp head movement.

What happens is that the sudden movement increases the pressure in the blood vessels in your eyes for a few moments. That triggers the nerves in your eyes, fooling your brain into thinking you're seeing spots of light.

Another way to make this happen is to press on your eyes with your fingers. (Close them first, of course. Can't be too careful about these things.) You'll see what appear to be patches of light on the inside of your eyelids. Try this in a darkened room for best results.

Both floaters and spots are harmless—usually. Sometimes, though, they're a sign of serious problems. If someone gave you a whack on the head and you saw a sudden shower of *dark* spots, that could mean a blood vessel in your eye had broken. Or maybe you're about to suffer a detached retina.[3] In both cases the spots actually could be tiny drops of blood, so please see a doctor. Luckily, detached retinas usually only happen when you're older.

[3]We talked about the retina on pages 10-11.

WHY DOES YOUR BODY JERK SOMETIMES WHEN YOU'RE FALLING ASLEEP?

It's likely you're just experiencing a condition known as **hypnagogic myoclonus** (hip-nuh-GAH-jik my-oh-KLOE-niss). Translated from the Latin, that means "twitches while falling asleep." Big help.

Scientists don't really know what causes sleep twitching. What's more, they don't much care, since nobody dies from it. Nice attitude, but that's the way scientists are.

The best guess is that sleep twitches are caused by slight noises or other disturbances. In fact, one way to trigger sleep twitching is to find someone who's nodding off in class and make a faint sound in their ear, or give them a gentle poke. (*Gentle* poke. We must be civilized about this.) Chances are they'll sit bolt upright and look around in surprise. Always a good way to liven up a dull day.

My guess is that sleep twitches are a carryover from the time when our ancestors lived in the wild. In those days you had to be careful lest the bad guys from the next cave get the drop on you. Any slight noise would cause you to become alert instantly.

HOW COME YOU GET A HEADACHE WHEN YOU EAT ICE CREAM TOO FAST?

The official medical term for this is "ice cream headache." Obviously there was some mistake. No self-respecting doctor would call an ailment by a name so simple any idiot could understand it. Any day now I expect to learn that "ice cream headache" has been renamed **hypothermic neuralgia** or something equally baffling.

No one is quite sure what causes an ice cream headache. One likely guess is that it happens when ice cream (or other cold stuff) causes the blood vessels near the roof of your mouth to contract (i.e., shrink) a bit. Since the blood can't flow through these vessels as quickly as before, it backs up into the head, causing the other blood vessels to stretch. Result: pain.

Ice cream headache is thought to be similar to another type of headache called **migraine** (MY-grane). Migraine headaches, which are very painful, strike some people again and again. The difference is that ice cream headaches are usually gone in a couple of minutes; migraines can be with you for hours. If you don't get them, count yourself lucky.

WHAT ARE THE DREAMS OF THE BLIND LIKE?

It all depends on when they became blind. If it happened after they were about seven or so, their dreams are similar to those of sighted people, at least at the beginning. It's a different story for people who've been blind from birth, or who became blind when very young. Since they've never known what it's like to see— or they've forgotten—they don't see anything in their dreams. Instead, they rely on the senses they have. Their dreams involve sounds plus the sensations of smell, touch, and taste.

The "plots" of the dreams of the blind usually aren't as elaborate as those of sighted people. Often they'll dream about the events of the previous day rather than about car chases or fighting bad guys. But don't feel sorry for blind people. A lot of sighted people (like me) can't remember what they dreamed about anyway.

Why are Oriental eyes different from European eyes?

Some people think Oriental eyes slant. Not true. But Orientals do have an extra flap of skin in front of the eyelids that makes their eyes appear narrower than European or African eyes. The flap of skin is called the **epicanthic** (eh-pih-KAN-thik) **fold**. (See illustration.)

Why is it there? One theory is that the epicanthic fold gives Orientals a natural pair of snow goggles, protecting their eyes against cold and glare.

Scientists believe the ancestors of today's Oriental peoples were trapped in Siberia by the glaciers during the last Ice Age, between 50,000 and 25,000 years ago. Siberia is the frigid northern part of Asia, now part of Russia.

To survive the cold, Orientals had to adapt or die. Their noses became flatter and less exposed to the wind, which made frostbite less likely. Their **nostrils** (the part of your nose that you breathe through) became narrower so that air could get warmed up more on the way into the lungs. Their faces also developed a layer of fat to keep in the heat.

Because of the epicanthic fold, Orientals' eyelids are thicker and have more fat, giving their eyes more protection. Having an extra outer eyelid also keeps snow and ice from building up on their inner eyelids. Finally, the fact that Oriental eyes are narrower protects them against glare from snow.

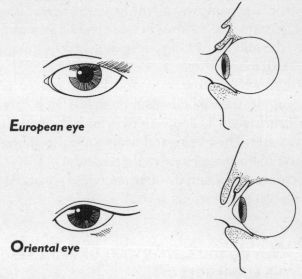

European eye

Oriental eye

The epicanthic fold gives the Oriental eye extra protection.

HOW DO ESKIMOS STAND THE COLD?

Hey, they *like* the cold. What they hate is the heat. No kidding. Some visitors to the Arctic claim Eskimos start complaining about how hot it is once the temperature gets above 40 degrees or so.

The fact is, Eskimos have adapted to the cold. Over many years of living in the Arctic their bodies have developed special ways of keeping warm.

The first is the way their bodies are shaped. Eskimos

tend to be short and squat, rather than tall and thin. This does two things. If you're short, your arms and legs (and for that matter, everything else in your body) are closer to that little heat pump we call the heart. So there's less danger of freezing. You've also got more padding around your **torso** (the middle part of your body), so your innards are protected, too.

Eskimos have other things that help them out as well. For example, their **metabolism** (meh-TAB-oh-liz-em) is set a little higher. That means they burn their food faster to stay warm. Their veins and arteries are also arranged to carry more warming blood to their hands.

So don't complain if you're short and squat. At least you'll never get frostbite.

WHY DO YOU ALWAYS WAKE UP RIGHT BEFORE THE ALARM GOES OFF?

A couple of things are at work here. The first part involves your own bodily alarm clock.

Everybody experiences **circadian** (sir-KAY-dee-en) **rhythms**. Circadian rhythms are changes in the way your body works over the course of a day. One of these rhythms involves body temperature.

Your body temperature usually is highest during the day and drops at night. It reaches its lowest point around 4 A.M. and then rises again. When it does, you begin to wake up. Around 6 or 7 A.M., even though you may not be fully alert, you're aware of what's going on around you.

Then something else happens. Many alarm clocks make a faint click a few moments before they sound the alarm. When you're half awake, you hear this click, even if you're not fully aware of it. Bingo, you're out of bed like a shot, before the alarm has a chance to go off. Fun it's not, but it *is* a good way to get the blood flowing first thing in the morning.

IF YOU KEEP YOUR EYES OPEN WHILE SNEEZING, WILL YOUR EYES POP OUT?

Truth is, you *can't* keep your eyes open when you sneeze. They snap shut by **reflex**. A reflex is something your body does automatically, without your having to think about it. For example:

MOM: Where are you going?
YOU: Nowhere.
MOM: What are you going to do?
YOU: Nothing.

See? Reflex.

Other reflexes include the way your leg jerks when the doctor hits your kneecap with that little hammer. Or a blink.

You can understand why swinging something at your eyes would cause the blink reflex, but sneezing? The best guess is that sneezing irritates the eyes, and shutting them relieves this. It's certainly not to keep your eyes from popping out.[4]

---

[4] Then again, David Feldman, author of *When Do Fish Sleep?*, quotes some quack as saying, "We close out eyes when sneezing to keep the eyes from extruding"—that is, popping out. Honestly, Dave, don't *encourage* these people.

How come whenever I go out into bright light I sneeze?

You say you don't have this problem? Well, a lot of people do—between one-sixth and one-quarter of the population, some say. They have what's known as **photic** (FOTE-ick) **sneeze reflex** ("sneeze reflex caused by light").

Photic sneeze reflex is probably inherited from your parents. What causes it? Nobody knows. (Amazing how much stuff nobody knows, isn't it?) What we do know is that the nerves for the eye and the nose run pretty close together. Some think what we've got here is a case of nerve signals getting crossed. If it bugs you . . . well, there's always brain surgery. But personally, I'd learn to live with it.

Why does the hair on your head keep growing while the hair on the rest of your body gets to a certain length and then stops?

Actually, the hair on your head *does* stop growing eventually. It just takes a lot longer.

Here's what happens. All the hair on your body has times when it's growing and times when it's not. When hair isn't growing, it's said to be **dormant**. After hanging around the **follicle** (FAHL-ih-kull) awhile (the follicle is the socket in your skin that the hair grows out of), the old piece of hair gets shoved out by a new hair pushing up from below. (See illustration.)

New hair pushing out old one from below.

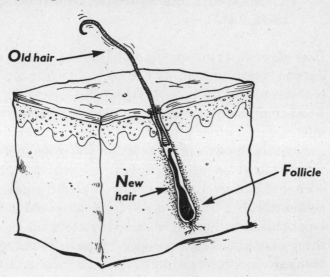

Old hair

New hair

Follicle

On most of your body, the hair grows only a short time before becoming dormant. As a result, it only gets to be maybe a half inch long.

But head hair grows for a much longer time—from two to six years. If you let it grow all that time, it could get two to three feet long. Maybe even longer. There's a woman in Massachusetts whose hair got to be 10½ feet long. (Obviously this is not somebody you want to let get into the bathroom ahead of you in the morning.)

Eventually, though, your head hair is going to stop growing—not all at once, of course, or you'd go bald when the hairs fell out. Each hair stays dormant for about three months, then gets pushed out by a new hair coming in from below. You lose maybe 70 to 100 hairs a day this way. If you're male, save them. By the time you're 40 you'll need all you can get.

CAN HAIR BECOME WHITE OVERNIGHT BECAUSE OF FRIGHT?

Lots of people think so, but it's hard to see how it could happen. Hair, after all, is not alive. Once it has been pushed out of the follicle, it's dead, dead, dead. Its color won't change unless you bleach or dye it. A sudden shock might turn new hair white, but it would be weeks before the hair had grown out enough that you would notice it.

So is sudden whitening just a myth? Maybe not entirely. Doctors tell of something called **diffuse alopecia areata** (dih-FYOOSE al-oh-PEE-sha air-ee-AH-tuh), a type of baldness that can be caused by stress, among other things. For some reason, alopecia primarily affects hairs with color, not gray or white ones. It can happen very suddenly.

Now, suppose a person with a mixture of white and normal hairs had a sudden shock and suffered alopecia. If only the normal (colored) hairs fell out, leaving just the white ones, it would seem as though the person's hair had suddenly turned white. I'm not saying this is what *always* happens when a person's hair turns "white from fright." But it might happen once in a while. (The rest of the time it probably doesn't happen at all.)

HOW COME YOUR EARS "POP" WHEN YOU RIDE IN A FAST ELEVATOR?

You're worried it's your eardrums bursting, right? Well, don't panic. Popping ears are a sign everything is under control. It's when your ears *don't* pop that you could be in trouble.

The problem you're dealing with here is air pressure. Air pressure gets lower the higher up you go. If it gets too low, your ears start to hurt. That's because the pressure

If the pressure inside the ear is greater than the pressure outside, the eardrum may become painfully distorted.

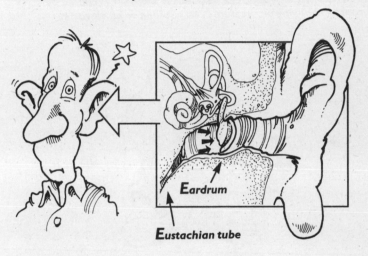

Eardrum

Eustachian tube

inside your head is so much higher than the pressure outside that it starts pushing on your cardrum. (See illustration.)

Luckily, there is a way to make the pressure equal. It involves something called the **eustachian** (yoo-STAY-shee-un) **tube**. This tube connects the space behind your eardrums to the nasal passage. When you swallow, the eustachian tube opens and air can flow back and forth, making the air pressure inside your head equal to the outside pressure.

But when you ride in a fast elevator, it's hard to swallow fast enough to keep up. You're better off trying something known as the **Vasalva technique**. Hold your nostrils closed with your thumbs, as shown in the illustration. Then try to blow through your nose as hard as you can.

The Vasalva technique can help relieve discomfort caused by rapidly changing air pressure in an airplane or an elevator.

This forces open the eustachian tube and makes the pressure equal. Your ears pop and you feel better. You also look like something of a geek, but this is one time when you want to put comfort before appearances.

WHERE DOES BELLY BUTTON LINT COME FROM?

Ah, the mysteries of nature. The answer is perfectly logical. You wear cotton undershirts, right? Lint comes off the cotton undershirts and winds up sticking to the sweat that collects in your belly button. Stop wearing undershirts—or stop sweating—and you'll never be troubled by belly button lint again.

HOW COME WE ALWAYS NOD OUR HEADS FOR "YES" AND SHAKE THEM FOR "NO"? DOES ANYBODY DO IT THE OPPOSITE WAY?

Obviously you've never visited Bulgaria. Bulgarians nod their heads for "no" and shake them for "yes." This makes traveling around in Bulgaria a real adventure. My advice, if you get nodding and shaking mixed up and the conversation really seems to be going off the rails, is to say, *Interesuvam se ot istoriyata na Balgariya* ("I am interested in the history of Bulgaria"). This will distract the Bulgarians long enough to let you escape.

Nodding and shaking your head are probably the most common gestures around the world for "yes" and "no," but there are lots of exceptions. In parts of Greece and Italy people say "no" by tossing their heads back and clucking their tongues. Eskimos supposedly nod for "yes" but wink for "no"—which is also confusing, since for many Americans a wink means "just kidding."

WHY DO WE SLEEP?

Another surprise—nobody really knows. You might think the answer would be obvious. We sleep to recharge our energy, right? Well, it's not that simple. Some people hardly ever sleep, and they seem to be fine. Finer, in fact, than some people who sleep a lot.

Some British scientists found a 70-year-old woman who slept an average of *one hour a night*. No catnaps during the daytime, either. Yet she was perfectly healthy and alert. Once she stayed awake for 56 hours straight, and then slept only an hour and a half. She still felt fine.

So why are the rest of us wasting eight hours a day (or more) in bed? Good question. Obviously we get pretty cranky if we *don't* sleep, but what exactly a nap does for us is a matter of debate. Here are some leading theories.

1. *Sleep gives the body time to recover from the stress of everyday life.* By the time night arrives, your **neurons** (NOOR-ons, "nerve cells") are shot. You need a break. During sleep, some scientists believe, your body repairs burnt-out brain cells and makes more of the special chemicals you need to help you think. This theory sounds reasonable, but it hasn't been proven yet.

2. *Sleep helps us save energy.* When you sleep, your body temperature drops a few degrees and you burn up less energy. That means you don't have to eat as much. Thousands of years ago, when we were all living in caves, getting food could be tough. You had to do a lot of scrounging—so much that if you were awake 24 hours a day, you'd have to be looking for food nonstop, just to keep your body supplied with energy. On the other hand, if you were asleep part of the time, you'd use less energy and you could take a break from eating once in a while.

3. *Sleep keeps us out of trouble.* No kidding. In prehistoric times, nighttime was when saber-toothed tigers and other dangerous creatures used to prowl about. So maybe we got into the habit of sleeping at night so we'd have less

chance of getting killed.

4. *Sleep helps us remember.* Sleep gives the brain time to sort out the day's events and put them into the right mental filing cabinets. It's true that things you learn right before going to sleep you remember better than things you learned at other times.

5. *Sleep helps us forget.* Some scientists say sleep helps you "unlearn" things, so your brain won't get too crowded with unneeded knowledge. (Not a problem for a lot of people I know.)

The whole thing is so confusing, I have half a mind never to sleep again. I'd probably be better off, too. Scientists say that people who sleep less than average (less than six hours a night) are more organized and efficient than everybody else. In other words, while you were moping around in bed this morning, some hotshot was out getting the jump on you. Something to think about next time you're tempted to catch another 40 winks.

WHAT CAUSES THE WHITE SPECKS ON YOUR FINGERNAILS?

Lots of things could cause white spots. Certain diseases, for instance. Or not enough zinc in your diet. But usually a white spot just means there's an air bubble trapped under your fingernail, or that the protein in your nail didn't form properly, or that you pinched the nail somehow and damaged it. (In the last case, you see a white mark for the same reason you see a white line in a piece of stiff plastic sheet when you bend it.)

White spots are more common in young people than adults. In most cases, they're nothing to worry about; in time they'll grow out, maybe even disappear on the way. If your fingernail turns *completely* white, on the other hand, that's a different story. See your doctor pronto.

What does it mean when someone has "perfect pitch"?

It's more than simply being able to stay on key, which any professional singer can do. People with perfect pitch don't need anybody to "give them the note." If you ask them to sing "G above middle C," for example, they'll be able to sing that exact note, without using a pitch pipe. Play a note—any note—and someone with perfect pitch will be able to identify it. In fact, they can even tell you if the piano (or whatever) is out of tune!

Perfect pitch isn't something you're born with. But you have to learn it when you're very young—say, starting at four years old. So it's a safe bet that if you haven't got perfect pitch now, you probably never will.

What good is perfect pitch? For the most part, not much. Even people who have perfect pitch admit it's not something you can use to impress girls on dates. A singer with perfect pitch may be asked to give the rest of the choir the proper note, but otherwise it doesn't have much practical use.

In fact, sometimes it can be downright annoying. If an ordinary musician is playing with an orchestra that's a little off-key, he'll probably never notice. A musician with perfect pitch, however, may find the experience almost painful.

Still, with proper training, perfect pitch can be a strange and wonderful gift. I once spoke to a professor of music with perfect pitch. He could read a piece of sheet music and create an exact performance of it in his mind, without ever hearing it played—even if it was a difficult piece involving many instruments.

Years had gone by before he'd heard some of his favorite tunes actually performed, but it didn't seem to bother him. He could create the music in his mind whenever he wished.

The professor was modest about his ability, but to me it seemed on a level with Michael Jordan's slam dunks. Clearly, your life won't be ruined if you don't have perfect pitch. But count yourself fortunate if you do.

CAN YOU REALLY BREAK GLASSES WITH YOUR VOICE?

Sorry to be a wimp about this, but I'm not sure. Lots of people, including some scientists, think opera singers can break glasses with their voices. But whether anybody has actually done it or not is another story.

Some people claim the famous singer Enrico Caruso, who lived around the turn of the century, could break glasses with his voice. But Caruso's wife later denied he had ever done such a thing.

Years ago the makers of Memorex recording tape (you remember, "Is it live or is it Memorex?") used to run television commercials showing glasses being broken.

They'd get Ella Fitzgerald to sing as loud as she could. Crack! A glass broke.

Then they'd play back the tape of Ella's singing and break another glass. This was supposed to prove how good Memorex tape was. (To me it mainly proved you should never wear glasses to an Ella Fitzgerald concert.)

Well, Ella *did* break glasses—but it turns out she had a little help. Her voice was **electronically amplified**. In other words, Memorex cheated.

But why would the glass break even with amplification? It's because of something known as **forced oscillation** (ah-sill-LAY-shun) **resonance** (REH-zuh-nents). Certain glasses, such as the expensive kind called leaded crystal, have a **natural frequency** (FREE-kwen-see) **of vibration**. That means when you hit them with a spoon, they ring with a certain note.

If you want to break a glass with your voice, first get one made of crystal. Now plunk it with a spoon. Remember the sound the glass makes. Then sing the *exact same note*. The glass will vibrate—that is, the sides will rapidly flex in and out. With luck, and an extremely loud voice, you'll find they flex so much the glass breaks. The folks at Memorex say the glasses they used would vibrate as much as a quarter inch just before breaking— pretty surprising considering how hard and solid glass seems to be most of the time.

Here's how it works. When you push your kid brother on a swing, you know that if you want to make him go as high as possible, you have to give him a shove just when he's swung back as far as he's going to go. Shove him hard enough and often enough, and in no time he'll be airborne.

Same deal, more or less, with singing. Only this time it's the sound vibration that's doing the shoving. The sound gives the vibrating glass a "boost" every time the sides of the glass get to the point of maximum flex. If the sound is loud enough the glass eventually will break.

Another example of forced oscillation resonance involves **suspension bridges**. They're the kind where the roadway is hung between two towers with cables, such as the Golden Gate Bridge in San Francisco.

In 1831 some soldiers in England discovered an interesting thing about suspension bridges. They were marching over one near the city of Manchester, keeping step in time to the swaying of the bridge. The interesting thing the soldiers discovered was that when you do this the bridge collapses. Ever since, soldiers have been told to break step when crossing bridges. No doubt about it, forced oscillation resonance is not something to mess with.

Do HAIR AND NAILS CONTINUE TO GROW FOR A TIME AFTER DEATH?

No, although they may seem to. In order to grow, hair and nail cells must be nourished by the blood. At death, the blood stops flowing and the hair and nails stop growing. They may appear to grow because the body dries out after death. The skin pulls away slightly from the hair and nails, letting more show—perhaps an extra ⅟₁₆ of an inch. So they *look* like they're growing. But they're not really.

Is it true we use only 10 percent of our brains?

Well, some people certainly aren't operating at 100 percent. But in general the answer is no—you use every part of your brain. Not every area at the same time, of course; they all do different things at different times. At any given moment, only about 5 percent of your brain cells are actually firing—that is, working. So in one sense this old saying is true. But as far as we know, there are no parts that never do *anything*.

It's a good thing. The brain is small and it's got a big job to do. What with algebra, computers, and programming the VCR, these days you need every brain cell you've got.

Why is some hair curly and some hair straight?

Because curly hair has a different **cross section** from straight hair. If you were to slice off a piece of curly hair and look at the end under a microscope, you'd see it was rather flat. The cross section of a straight hair, however, is round. (See illustration.)

Why should the cross section matter? Try this experiment. Can you make a flat piece of paper stand upright on a table by holding it at its bottom with just the tips of your thumb and forefinger? No—it curls right over, just like a curly hair does with its flat cross section.

But if you roll the paper into a cylinder, it's easy to make it stand up straight. A hair with a round cross sec-

Cross section of straight hair   **C**ross section of curly hair

tion stays straight for the same reason.

A cylindrical shape provides strength, so it's often used when it's important that something not bend. That's why you see cylindrical chimneys and cylindrical columns in buildings.

WHY ARE YAWNS CONTAGIOUS?

Nobody knows for certain.

The main problem is that nobody is sure why we yawn at all. Many people believe we yawn because our bodies are demanding more oxygen. Others say we yawn because it's too warm in the room.

I don't know who's right, but I do know this: If it's too warm or there's not enough oxygen around, not only do *you* want to yawn, so does everybody else in the room. So when you yawn, the power of suggestion is enough to trigger yawns in those nearby.

Until someone else comes up with a better theory, I'm sticking with this one.

WHY ARE SO MANY MORE PEOPLE RIGHT-HANDED THAN LEFT-HANDED?

This is a complicated subject, but it has a simple answer: We don't know. It would make a lot more sense if about *half* of us were left-handed, or if there were *no* left-handers, but when the percentage of left to right is 15–85 or 10–90 (estimates vary), it seems a little odd.

True, it's a lot easier to be right-handed these days. Righties are in charge and they've organized things to suit themselves. What with right-handed scissors, right-handed automobile gearshifts, and right-handed guns (if you're a lefty, the shell ejects right in front of your face), the world can be a dangerous place for a southpaw. Not surprisingly, they end up having more accidents. Does that mean there are fewer lefties because they've all been killed off? Thankfully, no—being left-handed isn't *that* dangerous.

It was once believed that everybody was right-handed to start with, but that lefties suffered some sort of brain damage during birth and had to switch. It is safe to say this theory was thought up by a right-handed scientist. You don't hear much about it anymore. But nobody has come up with a better explanation.

SO WHY DO THEY CALL LEFTIES "SOUTHPAWS," ANYWAY?

"Southpaw" dates back to the earliest days of baseball. A baseball diamond is always set up so the batter faces east. That way in the afternoon the batter won't have the sun in his eyes, and he'll be able to spot the pitch (and duck!) if it's about to hit him.

If the batter faces east, the pitcher has to face west. When he does, his left hand is on the south side of his body. So "southpaw" was a natural.

Is it true you should wait an hour after eating before swimming?

Water safety experts used to think so, but not anymore. Years ago they believed that stomach cramps caused by swimming on a full stomach were a leading cause of drowning. The cramps would cause you to double up in pain, you'd sink like a stone, and that would be the end of you.

Later research, however, showed that stomach cramps were rare. It's still not wise to swim long distances on a full stomach because you might become dangerously tired. But splashing around in the pool is harmless.

How do circus sword swallowers do it, anyway?

Believe it or not, they really do swallow the sword. The main problem is learning to relax the throat muscles and stop gagging. This takes weeks of practice, during which time there isn't much point eating lunch—it won't be down there long, if you take my meaning. But it can be done.

The sword doesn't cut the sword swallower's throat because its sides are dull. The point is usually sharp, but that's not a problem as long as the sword swallower doesn't swallow any swords long enough to poke him (or her) in the pit of the stomach. Some sword swallowers even swallow lighted neon tubes—quite a sight, I'm told.

The whole thing is incredibly dangerous even for the pros, so please don't try it . . . or when people say you speak with a forked tongue, they won't be kidding.

TIME

It's pathetic.

Sixty minutes in an hour, 24 hours in a day, 7 days a week, 365 days in a year. Thirty days hath September, April, June, and November. All the rest have 31, except February, which has 28. Except in leap year, when it has 29.

There's no doubt about it. Our system of timekeeping is a hodgepodge—maybe not as bad as 16½ feet to the rod and four bushels to the peck, but close. You can be sure if I had been in charge, things would have been organized a little differently.

Unfortunately, I wasn't. Nobody was, which is exactly the problem. All these oddball numbers were dreamed up at different times in different places for reasons that sounded good at the time. But taken together the whole thing makes no sense.

So why don't we change? Easier said than done, as we shall see. The question right now is, how did we get into this mess in the first place? Let's take it one step at a time.

WHY ARE THERE 60 SECONDS IN A MINUTE AND 60 MINUTES IN AN HOUR?

Blame the Babylonians. The Babylonians lived about 3,000 years ago in what is now Iraq. They thought 60 was a wonderful number. Why, only the Babylonians know. Best guess: They figured it was magic. (The ancients had a tendency to think everything was magic.)

Then again, maybe the Babylonians liked 60 because it could be evenly divided (no remainder) by so many smaller numbers: 2, 3, 4, 5, 6, 10, 12, 15, 20, and 30.

What's the big deal with dividing evenly? Simple—you avoid fractions, as in 10 divided by 3 equals 3⅓. This may be no big deal to you, but look at it from the point of view of Joe Babylonian. The guy lived in a mud hut and washed his underwear in the creek. He didn't have our modern advantages: high school, air conditioning, color television, calculators. When he saw a fraction, he freaked. So to him, 60 was great.

WHY ARE THERE 24 HOURS IN THE DAY?

To the ancients, 12 was another mystic number. It could be evenly divided by 2, 3, 4, and 6. (That's one of the reasons we still use dozens today.) Twenty-four hours is made up of two 12s—12 hours before noon, and 12 hours after.

WHY ARE THERE SEVEN DAYS IN A WEEK?

Probably because—stop me if you've heard this before—the ancients thought the number 7 was magic. Seven is a **prime number**. A prime number can't be evenly divided by anything except itself and one.

Another reason seven may have been chosen is that for thousands of years, before the invention of telescopes, people thought there were seven heavenly bodies, not counting stars: the sun, the moon, Mercury, Venus, Mars, Jupiter, and Saturn. (The three other planets we know of, Uranus, Neptune, and Pluto, weren't discovered till much later. Pluto wasn't found until 1930.)

Most people don't realize it, but the days of the week are named after the seven heavenly bodies:

1. *Sun*day.
2. *Mo(o)n*day.
3. Tuesday, "day of Tiw." (The ancients didn't spell very well.) Tiw was a Norse (Viking) god, the equivalent of the Roman god *Mars*. The Romans, you see, named the planets after their gods, and then named the days of the week after the planets. The Norse people took it one step further, substituting their own gods for the Roman gods who had days named after them.
4. Wednesday, "day of Woden." Woden was the Norse equivalent of the Roman god *Mercury*.
5. Thursday, "day of Thor." Thor was the Norse equivalent of the Roman god *Jupiter*.
6. Friday, "day of Frigg." There was a little mix-up here. Somebody thought Frigg was the Norse equivalent of the Roman goddess *Venus*. She wasn't; Freya was. But we won't tell anybody.
7. *Satur(n)*day.

There we go. Seven days, seven heavenly bodies. Surely that proves something.

WHY ARE THERE **365** DAYS IN A YEAR?

We can't blame this on our ancestors. This one's the fault of the universe.

Every time the earth spins around once, that's a day. Every time the earth goes around the sun once, that's a year. It just works out that in the time it takes the earth to go completely around the sun, our planet spins a little more than 365 times. So we have to have 365 days in a year. (See illustrations.)

But the worst of it is that the earth doesn't spin *exactly* 365 times in a year. It's more like 365¼. That's why we have to have **leap years** (years with an extra day) every four years—to keep the calendar lined up with the seasons.

Don't get it? It's like this. Right now, the coldest time of the year is December, January, and February. If there were no leap days, after a few hundred years went by, the coldest time of the year would be March, April, and May. Before you know it, it'd be snowing in August. So be thankful for leap days.

Noon   6 P.M.   Midnight   6 A.M.   Noon

I complete rotation of the earth = I day

April 1 (Spring)   **J**uly 1 (Summer)

1 year

January 1 (Winter)   **O**ctober 1 (Fall)

1 complete trip around the sun = 1 year

Why are there 12 months in a year?

There weren't always. Originally the Romans had only ten. They started their year in March and finished up in December. In fact, the names September, October, November, and December come from the Latin words for 7, 8, 9, and 10. (The Latin word that gave us October, eighth month, also gave us octave, eight notes.)

But wait a second, you're thinking. What did the Romans do between December and March? Beats me. Maybe they just sat around watching TV. The reason the Romans had a calendar in the first place was so they'd know when to plant, when to harvest, and so on. Since you couldn't grow anything between December and March, why bother with a calendar? So they didn't.

But finally around 700 B.C. a Roman king named Numa Pompilius got to thinking. We don't know exactly what he thought, but it was probably something along the lines of: "Boy, this is really stupid. The people of the future are going to think we were idiots if we don't fill in the space between December and March." So he invented January and February, thus saving the ancient world a lot of future embarrassment.

And that's why we have 12 months today. No kidding.[1]

WHY ARE THERE 30, 31, 28, OR 29 DAYS IN A MONTH?

This is the most scrambled part of the whole system, and it's all because of the Romans.

The Romans wanted a unit of time that was the length of a cycle of the moon, to make it easier to mark the passing of the seasons. (Our word "month" comes from "moon.") A cycle of the moon is the time it takes the moon to go from full to new (dark) and back to full. (See illustration.)

Full moon   Waning moon   New moon   Waxing moon   Full moon

1 lunar cycle = 29½ days

[1]OK, so maybe a *little* kidding.

As soon as the Romans started trying to work the moon into the calendar, though, they ran into trouble. Problem was, there wasn't an even number of days in a lunar cycle (a cycle is about 29½ days long). There also wasn't an even number of cycles in a year (there are about 12⅓).

But Numa Pompilius, the fellow who decided we were going to have 12 months in a year, wasn't one to get hung up on details. He boldly declared we were going to have 355 days in a year. True, he was a little off, but he didn't have the benefit of a college education.

Numa's next idea was that seven months should have 29 days, four should have 31 days, and one should have 28 days.

Why not split the difference and give all the months 30 days? Because the Romans were superstitious. They thought even numbers were bad luck.

Later on it dawned on somebody that the year had 365 days, not 355. So they added more days to some months. But we still wound up with different months having different numbers of days.

Which brings us to our next question.

ISN'T THERE A BETTER WAY?

Of course. Two hundred years ago, the leaders of the French Revolution decided to reform the system of measurement.

So they did. Amazingly, some of the reforms actually worked. You've heard of the metric system? The French invented it. To Americans, who still have to work with feet and yards and acres and other old-fashioned measures, the metric system just seems like one more set of numbers to have to learn.

But Europeans love it. The metric system is simple— 10 millimeters to the centimeter, 100 centimeters to the meter, 1,000 meters to the kilometer. You can learn the whole thing in about five minutes.

The French tried to do the same thing for timekeeping. *That* didn't work out quite so well.

They started with the "decimal second." One hundred decimal seconds made a decimal minute; 100 decimal minutes made an hour. There were 10 hours for each half of the day—20 hours per day in all. Ten days made a week, and three weeks made a month of 30 days. Twelve 30-day months plus five leap days (they called them "complementary days") made a year.

During the French Revolution, the new government decreed that the 12-hour clock would be replaced with a 10-hour clock. It was supposed to make timekeeping less confusing. It didn't.

People tried to make the new timekeeping system work. They even made special clocks with both 10-hour and 12-hour dials. (See illustration.)

But it didn't help. After 13 baffling years, they gave up and went back to the old system. The new way was just too confusing. Besides, what fun was it having a weekend every 10 days?

That's why we're stuck with the old system today: it's too much trouble to change it.

Why are there time zones?

You know what time zones are, right? Say you're in Boston, in the Eastern Time Zone, and it's 5 o'clock. In Chicago, in the Central Time Zone, it's 4 o'clock. In

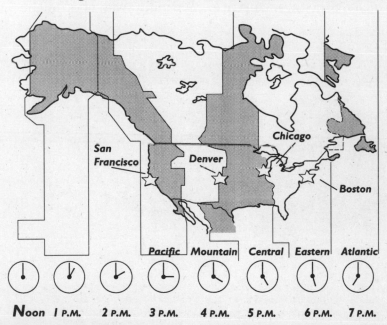

Denver, in the Mountain Time Zone, it's 3 o'clock, and in San Francisco, in the Pacific Time Zone, it's 2 o'clock.

Why can't the time be the same everywhere? Because the world is round, that's why.

Look at the drawing. Say you live in Dinkburg. The sun is directly overhead, so you decide it's high noon—12 o'clock. Meanwhile, a quarter of the way around the world, in Hicktown, the sun is low in the sky. And on the other side of the planet, in Dudville, it's pitch dark. If you decide to make it noon everywhere, the folks in Hicktown and Dudville are going to be mighty peeved.

One way to handle this time business is to let each town say, okay, when the sun is directly overhead, that'll be high noon for *us*. The rest of you guys can have your own time.

For many years, people did just that. In City A it might be noon, and in City B, 300 miles away, noon might

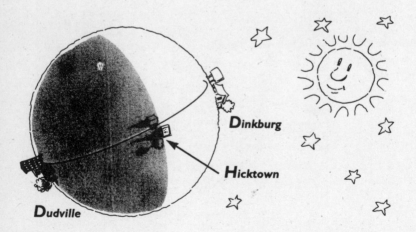

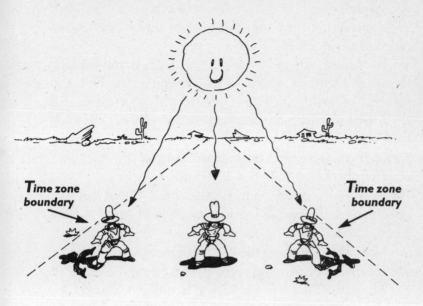

Old time (before standardization)

12:25 P.M. **N**oon 11:35 A.M.

New time (after standardization)

Noon **N**oon **N**oon

happen 17 minutes later. In City C, a little farther on still, noon might come 25 minutes after noon in City A.

That was fine when people didn't have much to do with folks in distant cities. But once high-speed methods of travel and communication were invented, life started getting more complicated.

Things were especially bad for the railroads. Suppose you're a railroad engineer and you're trying to keep to a schedule. Think how confused you'd be if you had to reset your watch every time you came to a different town! But 110 years ago, before there were time zones, that's what railroad engineers had to do.

Eventually the railroads got tired of this and decided to set up a simpler system of timekeeping. In 1884, the railroad bosses divided the country into four zones. All the towns within each zone had the same time, and each zone was exactly one hour different from the neighboring zones. If you were traveling across country, you reset your watch only three times, not 200 times.

Eventually other countries adopted the American system, and the whole world was divided into 24 time zones.

Not all countries made the change right away. Some did it only recently. And some places never did get with the program. Take Newfoundland in eastern Canada, for instance. When it's noon in Montreal, it's 12:30 in Newfoundland. A little confusing, but nowhere near as bad as it was in the old days.

WHICH IS CORRECT: 12 MIDNIGHT A.M. OR 12 MIDNIGHT P.M.?

Neither. That's because midnight doesn't belong either to the day before or the day after. Midnight is the dividing line *between* days, just as the present is the dividing line between the future and the past. So the proper thing to say is 12 midnight, period.

Twelve noon works the same way—it's neither A.M. nor P.M. Just 12 noon, period. Think about it. P.M. stands for "post meridiem," Latin for "after noon." Does it make sense to say "12 after noon"? Of course not. Try popping this one on a teacher sometime. Drives 'em nuts.

Did they really make somebody sit there for 24 hours to do all those "at the tone, the time will be . . . " recordings on the telephone?

Well, not exactly. But years ago, before recording devices were invented, somebody *did* have to sit there reciting the time—not just once, but every day.

Originally you could just call up the operator and ask what time it was. But that was back when there were only a few phones in the whole country and the operators didn't have much to do. Eventually, when business picked up, the operators got too busy for such things.

So instead the phone company started a special time service. You'd call a number and you'd get some poor woman sitting at a microphone calling off the time every 15 seconds—probably the worst job in history. Half an hour at a stretch was all most people could stand. Then they'd get a break and somebody fresh would take over.

Fortunately for all concerned, science marches on. Eventually tape-recording equipment was invented. Someone came up with a playback machine that enabled the time lady to record the hours, minutes, and seconds separately—one set of numbers each. In other words, she recorded the hours from 1 to 12, the minutes from zero to 59, and finally the seconds in 10-second jumps from zero to 50. Later, the playback device mixed them together to create the message you hear.

A similar device is used today, only the words are recorded on a magnetic drum instead of tape.[2] The same type of machine is used for sports results, Dial-A-Joke, and those dumb call-in services they're always advertising on MTV. The march of progress can be a mixed blessing.

WHEN DOES THE 21ST CENTURY BEGIN—AT MIDNIGHT ON JANUARY 1, 2000, OR MIDNIGHT ON JANUARY 1, 2001?

You probably thought that on New Year's Eve of 1999, instead of saying to people, "Hey, I'll see you next year," you could say, "I'll see you next *century*." Well, there's one small problem. The 21st century doesn't start until the year 2001. The year 2000 is still part of the 20th century.

"How can this be?" you ask. "Doesn't the century automatically change when you go from the 1900s to the 2000s?"

In a word, no. Think about it this way. Our present calendar started with the year 1 (there wasn't a year 0).

A century is always 100 years long. If the calendar started in the year 1, the first century wasn't over until the end of the year 100. That means the *second* century started on January 1 of the year 101.

If the second century started in the year 101, the third started in 201, and so on up the line until the 21st century, which starts in 2001. Some people refuse to believe that. But facts are facts.

[2]Two drums, actually. One has hours and minutes on it, the other has seconds.

IF YOU WERE BORN IN LEAP YEAR ON FEBRUARY 29, DOES THAT MEAN YOU ONLY HAVE A BIRTH-DAY ONCE EVERY FOUR YEARS?

This foolish idea never seems to go away. The short answer is no, you have a birthday every year, just like everybody else. In nonleap years it just happens to fall on February 28.

Some people—some pretty annoying people— object to this. "But you were born on the *29th*," they say. "Therefore, you have to *celebrate* on the 29th. If there isn't a 29th, you can't celebrate."

Wrong. A birthday marks the fact that you are one year older. A year is the time it takes the earth to make one complete revolution around the sun. This takes about 365¼ earth days—to be exact, 365 days, 6 hours, 9 minutes, and 9½ seconds.

Suppose you were born a half second after midnight on February 29, 1976. Your first birthsecond (just like your first birthday, only a lot more precise) occurs exactly one year later, at 6:09:10 A.M. on February 28, 1977. So you would properly celebrate your birthday on February 28.

Your second and third birthseconds would also fall on February 28. But your fourth would fall on February 29— that is, the next occurrence of leap day. So you should celebrate your birthday on the 28th every year except leap year, when you should celebrate on the 29th.

Here's a chart to prove I'm right. Let's assume two babies were born: Baby Albert at ½ second after midnight on February 29, 1976, and Baby Betty at ½ second after midnight on March 1, 1976. Here's where their birthseconds occur during the first four years:

	Baby Albert	Baby Betty
Time of birth	12:00:00.5 A.M. Feb. 29, 1976	12:00:00.5 A.M. Mar. 1, 1976
1st birthsecond **(1 year old)**	6:09:10 A.M. Feb. 28, 1977	6:09:10 A.M. Mar. 1, 1977
2nd birthsecond **(2 years old)**	12:18:19.5 A.M. Feb. 28, 1978	12:18:19.5 A.M. Mar. 1, 1978
3rd birthsecond **(3 years old)**	6:27:29 P.M. Feb. 28, 1979	6:27:29 P.M. Mar. 1, 1979
4th birthsecond **(4 years old)**	12:36:38.5 A.M. Feb. 29, 1980	12:36:38.5 A.M. Mar. 1, 1980

Baby Betty properly celebrates her birthday on March 1 of each year. Baby Albert, the leap year baby, celebrates his on February 29 during leap years, but February 28 the other three years. If you're a leap year baby, too, go ahead and light those candles.

WHY DO OLD CLOCKS HAVE PENDULUMS?

A pendulum isn't just for decoration; it's what enables the clock to keep time.

Four hundred years ago, Galileo Galilei, the famous

Italian scientist, saw an altar lamp swinging back and forth in church. He noticed that even though the distance the lamp traveled on each swing decreased, the **period** of the swing—that is, the time it took the lamp to make one

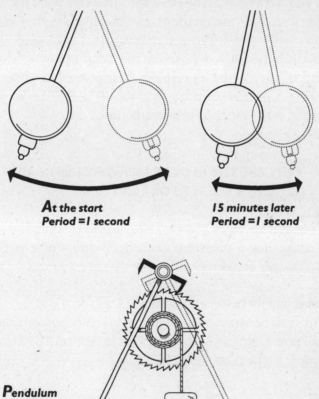

At the start
Period = 1 second

15 minutes later
Period = 1 second

Pendulum

Weight

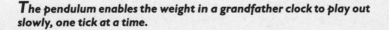

The pendulum enables the weight in a grandfather clock to play out slowly, one tick at a time.

full trip back and forth—stayed the same. If a swing took two seconds at the beginning, it still took two seconds 15 minutes later. Galileo proved this by timing the lamp with his pulse.

Pendulums, which operate the same way, were the key to inventing the **escapement**, the mechanism that regulates a clock's speed. Old grandfather clocks use weights to make the hands move. To make the weight play out slowly and regularly, the pendulum swings back and forth, allowing a gear to slip by one tooth (tick!) at a time (tock!). So the clock keeps steady time.

WHY ARE THE CLOCKS AND WATCHES IN ADVERTISEMENTS ALL SET FOR 8:20?

They're not always. Often they're set for 10:10. Either setting makes for a pleasantly balanced arrangement that doesn't cover up the manufacturer's name printed on the face.

It is widely believed that the clocks and watches are set for 8:20 because that's when Abraham Lincoln died. That's nonsense. Lincoln was shot a little after 10 P.M. and died at 7:30 the next morning.

THE 4 EARTH

Can you really use a dowsing rod to find water?

You've probably heard about people who claim they can find water underground with a special stick or a bent wire or some other device. This is called "dowsing" or "water witching." In the most common method, you walk around with a stick shaped like a Y, with your hands on the two branches and the main stem pointed ahead of you. When the main stem suddenly points down, supposedly you've found water.

Does this really work?

Does Michael Jordan need elevator shoes?

Take it from me, dowsing is an illusion. It's not that dowsers are trying to cheat people. Most of them probably think dowsing actually works. But that doesn't mean anything is actually happening.

You can prove this with a simple experiment. Get a yardstick and tie a string to the middle of it. Adjust the string so the yardstick balances. Then tie the other end of the string to a broomstick hung between the backs of two chairs. (See illustration.)

Now shove a bucket of water under the yardstick.

If dowsing really worked, the yardstick should be pulled toward the bucket of water. It doesn't, and it isn't.

Does the yardstick suddenly plunge down toward the water? Of course not. *That's because there's no attraction between wood and water.*

This experiment was first performed 300 years ago. So why do people still believe in dowsing? Because dowsing *looks* like it works.

Here's what happens. A dowsing "expert" walks around a field until suddenly his dowsing rod points earthward. He marks the spot, hands the dowsing rod to one of his friends, and says, "Here, you try."

Let's call the friend Joe. Trying to be cool, Joe holds the rod as he was told, then walks around the field. Sure enough, when he gets to the spot the "expert" marked, the rod quivers and plunges down! Hey, dowsing works, right?

Not so fast. What really made the stick point down was the power of suggestion.

You have to hold the dowsing rod in a funny way. It's actually under tension, like the spring in a mousetrap. If you relax your hands slightly, bingo, the stick points downward.

When Joe walks around with the dowsing rod, he wants to succeed, to prove he's as smart as his friend. (Ha!) When he gets near the spot his friend marked, he relaxes his hands a little, without meaning to. Sure enough, the stick points down.

Does all this sound farfetched? It isn't. In a laboratory years ago scientists had people whose arms were wired up with measuring devices lie down on cots. Then the scientists told the people to *think* about raising their arms, but *not to actually do so*. In almost every case, the instruments showed the people raised their arms a tiny bit without realizing it. Much the same thing happens with dowsing rods.

To prove it's the power of suggestion that made the dowsing rod point down, you could blindfold Joe. He could walk all over, and chances are the rod would plunge down at some point along the way. But it's very unlikely it would happen at the same spot that the expert dowser marked in the first place.

"Now hold on," dowsing buffs object. "When people drill where dowsers tell them, often they find water."

Well, sure. In most of the country, you'd have a tough time digging anywhere and *not* finding water, if you went deep enough. Water is all over the place.

When water seeps into the ground, it sinks until it gets

down to a layer of stone or hard clay that prevents it from going any farther. There it collects and spreads out, just like water at the bottom of a bottle full of sand. You could dig a well *anywhere* in an area like this and you'd hit water. So why do people still believe in dowsing? I don't know. But I'm not complaining. As long as they do, they'll still need guys like me to write books like this.

How do we know the earth is round?

Easy—because it looks round in the pictures the astronauts took. But maybe you had a slightly more challenging question in mind, such as: How would we know the

Proof that the earth is round #1: Ships seem to disappear over the horizon.

earth was round if we couldn't view it from space?

Way #1. Grab your old man's binoculars and go to the beach. Check out one of the boats heading out to sea. See how it sinks below the horizon, first the hull, then the cabin, then the sail? See how the Coast Guard helicopter rushes over to rescue all the people before they drown? Whoa, bad example. Look at that *other* boat sinking below the horizon. That's because it's sailing out of sight past the curvature of the earth, proving that the earth is round. (See illustration.)

Way #2. Go out in the country at night and look at the stars. Find the North Star, the brightest star in the sky.[1] All the stars in the sky appear to rotate around the North Star, because it's directly[2] over the North Pole.

Now walk due south 5,000 miles. As you walk, notice how the North Star sinks steadily lower in the sky. When you get to the equator, the North Star will be barely visible above the horizon. When you get *south* of the equator, you won't be able to see the North Star at all.

What's more, you'll see **constellations** (star clusters) that normally aren't visible from the northern half of the world, such as the Southern Cross, rising in the south. This would only happen if the earth were round. (See illustration.)

Way #3. Wait for a lunar eclipse. A lunar eclipse is

---

[1]You can't find it? Not to worry. Find the Little Dipper. The North Star is the last star in the handle. You can't find the Little Dipper either? Okay, find the *Big* Dipper. Anybody can find the Big Dipper. Look for the two stars that form the front of the dipper. Count out five dipper-lengths or so in the direction the two stars are pointing. See that bright star? That's the North Star.

[2]Well, almost directly.

Proof that the earth is round #2: At the North Pole, the North Star is
directly overhead . . .

. . . but in most of the United States, the North Star is midway
between the horizon and overhead. South of the equator, the North
Star can't be seen at all.

Proof that the earth is round #3: The earth casts a round shadow on the moon during lunar eclipses.

a darkening of the moon that occurs when the earth gets between the sun and the moon and casts a shadow. (See illustration.) The shadow is always round; therefore, the earth is round. True, maybe it's only round the way a plate is round, as opposed to a bowling ball. But you have to start somewhere.

Way #4. This is the Way of Philosophy. That means we sit around and think about it. First thought: The sun and the moon are round, right? So why should the earth be different?

Second thought: Go blow a soap bubble. It's spherical, right? Soap bubbles are round because a sphere (ball) has the least amount of surface for a given amount of volume. In other words, a ball is the most *efficient* shape. To put it still another way, the easiest thing for a soap bubble to be is round.

So it stands to reason that if the earth started out as a glob of lava floating in space, eventually it would pull itself into a ball, just like a soap bubble.

Still not convinced? Tell you what. You prove it's *flat*.

WHY IS THE SKY BLUE?

First an Amazing Fact. Did you ever wonder what color sunlight was? You'd probably guess it was yellow or white. But actually sunlight is made up of all the colors mixed together.

To prove this, you need something called a **prism** (PRI-zem). A prism is a piece of glass with flat surfaces ground into it. There are two ways to get one: (1) pay megabucks to buy one from a scientific supply house, or (2) steal one from Mom, assuming she has one of those lamps with crystal doodads hanging off it. (The crystal doodads are prisms.) The second approach is easier unless Mom is the excitable type.

Hold the prism up to the sun and look at the shadow it makes on the ground or the wall. The prism's shadow will be outlined with red, green, yellow, and blue. The prism has **refracted**—that is, bent—the light, breaking it into all the colors of the rainbow.

When light travels from the sun to us, it has to go through the earth's atmosphere. Most of the sunlight goes straight through, but some of it bounces off the particles of air. This is called **scattering**. (See illustration.) For complicated reasons I'm not going to explain right now

(you'll thank me for this someday), the blue part of the sunlight is scattered the most. It rattles around the sky for a while and finally heads down to you.

So here's the picture. You've got white light coming at you in a straight line from the sun, and you've got blue light coming at you from all directions. Thus the sun looks whitish-yellow and the rest of the sky looks blue.

If the blue light didn't bounce, the sun would still be bright, but the rest of the sky would be black. That's what happens on the moon, where there isn't any atmosphere to scatter the sunlight.

There. Now when *your* kid asks you why the sky is blue, you'll know what to say.[3]

[3]You'll say, "Here, kid, read this book."

WHY DOES THE SUN LOOK RED AT SUNRISE AND SUNSET, BUT WHITISH-YELLOW THE REST OF THE DAY?

At sunrise and sunset, when the sun is low in the sky, its light has to pass through the atmosphere lengthwise to reach us, rather than shining straight down. (See illustration.)

So much blue light is scattered out of the direct beam during its long journey that all that's left is red. (Well, it isn't *all* that's left. But there's more red than anything else.) So the sun *looks* red.

How soon is California going to fall into the ocean?

Not soon enough for some people. (Don't worry, they're just envious.) But let's get clear on one thing. The problem isn't that California is *sinking*, it's that it's *sliding sideways*—toward the Aleutian Islands, off the coast of Alaska. Do you know what the weather is like in the Aleutian Islands? Rotten, that's what. But California won't arrive there for 50 million years, so you don't have to break out the mukluks[4] just yet.

The "seam" in California (the crack where the two parts are sliding by one another) is called the San Andreas Fault. The west side of the fault is sliding past the east side at the rate of two inches per year.

This is important for several reasons. For one thing, if you're putting down carpet in California, you definitely don't want to staple any over the San Andreas Fault. More important, the two parts of the state don't slide past each other smoothly. Instead, they get snagged, like when you're trying to get past a tree in the forest and a branch catches on your pants.

What happens next? The same thing that sometimes happens when you try to get your pants leg loose. You tug and tug until it breaks loose and you topple over backward. In California, as the two pieces of the state try unsuccessfully to get past one another, the pressure builds up more and more. Then blammo, something snaps and it's earthquake city. Unfortunately for Californians, that could happen a lot sooner than 50 million years.

[4]Eskimo boots.

How many people have lived on Earth since the dawn of time?

Between 69 billion and 110 billion, depending on whom you ask. Obviously, figuring out stuff like this is not an exact science.

Back in 60,000 B.C., people were more concerned about not getting eaten by the local wildlife than they were about keeping count of the population. Also, if you go really far back, our ancestors start getting a bit too monkeylike for some people's tastes, and you get into arguments over who to count as human and who to leave out. But no matter how you figure it, a lot of people have lived on this planet.

Do bathtub drains go down counter-clockwise in the Northern Hemisphere and clockwise in the Southern Hemisphere?

Only if you're a *very* sloppy housekeeper. You don't see the connection? You will. But first some more Amazing Facts.

Forgetting bathtub drains for the moment, there are a few things that always go counterclockwise in the Northern Hemisphere and clockwise in the Southern. Hurricanes and tornadoes, for instance. Why? It's a little complicated to explain, but it all has to do with the rotation of the earth. We call this fact about spinning the **Coriolis effect**.

You can see how somebody might think that the

Coriolis effect applies to a bathroom drain. But tornadoes and hurricanes are huge; bathtub drains are tiny. Does the Coriolis effect work on small things as well as on large ones?

To find out, a scientist at the Massachusetts Institute of Technology did an experiment. He got a large round tub with a drain in the center and filled it with water, pointing the hose so that the water swirled in a *clockwise* direction—opposite the Coriolis effect. Then he drained the tub and watched what happened.

He found that if he pulled the plug right after filling, the water drained in a clockwise direction. This meant that the way the water drained was a result of the way it had been filled.

If he waited 24 hours, however, the water drained in a counterclockwise direction. This meant that the filling motion had quieted down enough that the Coriolis effect could take over.

So the way the water goes down the drain depends on the way you filled the tub—*unless you let the water sit in the tub all day*. In other words, the only people in the Northern Hemisphere who can be sure their tubs will drain in a counterclockwise direction are those with no sense of proper bathroom habits. No one, in other words, who could possibly be reading this book.

WHY IS THE SEA SALTY?

There used to be a wonderfully simple answer to this question. Too simple, it turns out.

The old explanation was that sea salt is made up of minerals that are washed off the land and into rivers by rain. The rivers flow into the sea, where they deposit their load of salt.

When water in the oceans **evaporates** (turns to vapor) and floats into the atmosphere, it leaves the salt behind. The water vapor forms rain clouds that float over the land, and the cycle starts over again.

The problem with this theory is that it suggests the oceans should be getting steadily saltier. But they're not. It's believed the saltiness of the oceans has been the same for many millions of years.

So where *did* the salt come from? Scientists aren't sure. But they have a good guess.

Salt is made up of two kinds of atoms: **sodium** (SO-dee-um) and **chlorine** (KLOR-een). Scientists think the sodium, along with a lot of other chemicals, is washed into the oceans from the land, as in the old theory. The chlorine is belched up from cracks in the ocean floor and from underwater volcanoes. The two chemicals combine to form salt.

Why doesn't the sea get steadily saltier? Because sodium and chlorine are not only being put into the ocean, they're also being taken out. They combine with other chemicals to form **sediments**, claylike materials that sink to the bottom of the sea and get packed into the ocean floor.

The amount of salt leaving the ocean equals the amount being added, so the overall saltiness remains the same. In an age of constant change, it's nice to know there's one thing you can depend on.

Do TREES EVER DIE OF OLD AGE?

Not in the sense that humans do. Humans have a **fixed life span**—they can live to a certain age, but no longer. Today the average person can expect to live to be about 74 years old. A few folks live into their 90s and beyond. But many scientists believe it's physically impossible for humans to live beyond 120 years or so. (The story in the Bible about **Methuselah** [meh-THOO-zeh-lah] living to be 969 is surely exaggerated.)

All trees die eventually, but they don't seem to have a fixed life span like we do. The average tree may be said to live a certain number of years, depending on what kind of tree it is. Most trees are killed at a fairly early stage by accidents, disease, insects, and so forth. But some live much longer.

The best example of this is the **bristlecone** (BRISS-ul-cone) **pine**. Most bristlecone pines live to be 200 to 375 years old. But some have been discovered in California that are more than 4,000 years old.

How can trees live so long? Mainly because they're much less complicated than we are. Humans and animals have brains that control their activities. When your brain dies, you die.

But trees, like all plants, are simpler. They don't have brains. Many parts of a tree can die without killing the tree as a whole. In fact, much of a normal, healthy tree is dead—the wood in the center, for example. The only living parts of a tree are a thin layer beneath the bark called the **cambium** (KAM-bee-um), plus the leaves and the tips of the roots and branches.

All that's left living on those ancient bristlecone pines in California are a few strands of cambium and some leaves. But year after year they keep struggling on. Probably they'll still be doing so long after we're gone.

IF...

IF YOU WERE IN AN ELEVATOR AND THE CABLES SNAPPED, COULD YOU SAVE YOURSELF BY JUMPING UPWARD AT THE LAST SECOND?

Wouldn't hurt to try, I guess, and Lord knows I'm not going to tell you how to spend the last 10 seconds of your life. But the chances of it working are pretty slim. Let's suppose your elevator is falling downwards at 40 miles per hour, or nearly 60 feet per second. Now suppose you jump up at the last moment. How fast do you think you're going to go? Forty miles per hour? Fat chance.

Let's be generous and say you could jump up at 10 miles per hour. Forty miles an hour *down* minus 10 miles per hour *up* leaves you going 30 miles per hour down. In short, no matter what you do, you're going to come out of this looking like a pizza.

But don't get too alarmed. There isn't just one elevator cable holding you up, there are several—often five or six. Any one cable could support the weight of the entire elevator. If by some evil miracle all the cables did snap, the elevator is also equipped with brakes that would grab the sides of the shaft. If the brakes failed, too, some elevators have giant springs at the bottom. So maybe you'd just bounce.[1]

---

[1]Other elevator shafts have giant plungers filled with oil at the bottom. So maybe you'd just sort of ooze.

If that doesn't work—well, they'll be scraping you off the floor with a putty knife. But look on the bright side: at least you won't have to make a lot of stops on the way down.

IF ALL THE PEOPLE IN CHINA JUMPED OFF CHAIRS AT THE SAME TIME, WOULD THE EARTH BE THROWN OUT OF ITS ORBIT?

I once spent the whole day with my brother-in-law trying to figure this out. (Don't worry, I get paid for doing this.) The answer we came up with was that the total overall thud made by one billion falling Chinese would have roughly the same force as 500 tons of TNT.[2]

Five hundred tons of TNT would give you a pretty decent explosion, no question about it. However, the earth weighs 6 sextillion, 588 quintillion tons. In other words, you've got

Tons of TNT: 500
Tons of earth: 6,588,000,000,000,000,000,000.

You get the picture: don't worry about it.

---

[2]One guy did complain that we screwed up the arithmetic, claiming that it would be only 70 tons. My feeling is, what's 430 tons between friends?

IF SOMEBODY DUG A HOLE ALL THE WAY THROUGH THE CENTER OF THE EARTH AND YOU FELL IN, WHAT WOULD HAPPEN?

The simplest answer is to watch where you're going so you don't have to worry about stuff like this. But suppose you got careless one morning. What then?

The first thing to realize is that the center of the earth is partly **molten** (melted) rock. If you fall into that, they'll bury what's left of you in a mason jar.

But just for fun, let's suppose they shoved a fireproof pipe through the molten rock, to keep it out of the way. And suppose they gave you a couple of ice cubes and a fan on the way down to keep you cool. *Then* what would happen?

Well, first it's necessary to ignore the effect of friction from the air. (You'll see why in a minute.) Next, focus your mind on the following Weird Fact: At the center of the earth, you would weigh absolutely nothing. That's because there would be an equal amount of the earth's mass on all sides of you. The forces of gravity pulling you in one direction would be canceled out by the forces of gravity pulling you in the opposite direction. Net weight: zip.[3]

When you first fell into the hole, the force of gravity would make you fall faster and faster. But as you got toward the center of the earth, your weight would decrease, and you'd stop speeding up.

At the center you'd weigh nothing, but you'd have so much speed built up you'd coast past the center and out toward the far end. From then on, most of the earth's mass

[3]The center of the earth is obviously Dieter's Heaven.

would be *behind* you. That would gradually cause you to
slow down.

You'd fall all the way through the earth until you
reached the very edge of the rim on the far side of the hole,
8,000 miles away from where you started. You'd pause
briefly (just as well—you'd be in the middle of the Pacific
Ocean), then start to fall back down the way you'd just
come.

You'd fall all the way through, right back to the place
you started, where the process would start all over again.
This would continue until the end of time. (See illustration.)

But remember, we said we were going to ignore the
effects of air friction. In reality, you *can't* ignore the effects
of air friction. Air friction would slow you down and prevent you from going as fast as you could if the air weren't
there. You'd shoot past the center of the earth, but you

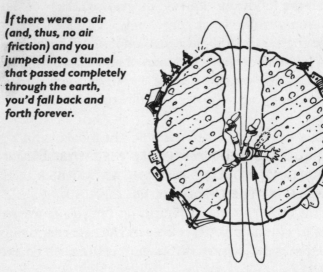

If there were no air
(and, thus, no air
friction) and you
jumped into a tunnel
that passed completely
through the earth,
you'd fall back and
forth forever.

If there were air, eventually you'd come to a stop in the middle of the earth.

wouldn't get all the way out to the other side before you started to fall back.

Once you did fall back, you'd zoom past the center of the earth again, but you wouldn't get back to your starting point before slowing down and reversing direction yet again. And so it would go—you'd swing back and forth, going less and less distance each time, until finally you wound up at a standstill in the center. (See illustration.)

Doesn't sound like much fun. Take my advice and watch out for those holes.

IF YOU DROPPED A PENNY OFF THE EMPIRE STATE BUILDING, WOULD IT BE GOING AS FAST AS A BULLET BY THE TIME IT HIT THE GROUND?

Somebody told me this when I was a kid, and I believed it. But eventually I wised up. Having performed various complicated mathematical maneuvers, I can tell you that under the best of conditions, the penny would be going about 190 miles per hour. The slowest bullet goes about 550 miles per hour, almost three times as fast.

Another fact to consider is that tall buildings are often surrounded by **updrafts** (winds that blow up). These would slow down anything that was falling. I've heard that the updrafts around the Empire State Building are so strong you can put a paper cup upside down outside your window and it'll just float there.

So your penny is not going to do all that much damage. On the other hand, there's still a chance it might give somebody a pretty good rap on the noggin. So promise me you won't try it.

WHAT WOULD HAPPEN IF THE EARTH WERE TO FALL INTO A BLACK HOLE?

A black hole is a wad of stuff with such incredibly strong gravity that even light cannot escape. Black holes usually result when giant stars run out of gas and collapse into tiny clumps of superheavy stuff. I say "usually" like it happens all the time, but the truth is nobody has ever actually seen a black hole—since no light can get out of them, they're invisible. But scientists are pretty sure they exist.

The gravity of black holes is so strong that everything in the neighborhood, including planets, gets sucked in. However, (1) since only very big stars can get to be black holes, and (2) since our wimpy sun is too small to qualify, death by black hole won't be our planet's fate. We'll just get torched when the sun goes into "red giant" stage, which happens to all old stars eventually. Luckily, this won't happen for another few billion years.

But suppose you were out walking the dog and a black hole magically appeared. (It's my book. Anything can happen.) What would it be like?

It'd be no day at the beach, that's for sure. You'd have two problems: intense radiation and tidal forces. The pull of gravity at one end of you would be so much stronger than at your other end that your body would be ripped apart.

But suppose you were lucky and somehow survived. Then what? Well, there's no way to know for sure, but some folks think you might get spat out at a different place in space and time by way of something called a "wormhole." This is too complicated to explain now. But there's an outside chance that someday it may be possible to travel through time.

WHAT IF THE EARTH WERE HIT BY A BIG METEORITE FROM SPACE?

I've got news for you, kids—every once in a while the earth *does* get hit by big meteorites from space.[4] Every once in a while the Cubs win the NL East,[5] too. But neither event happens very often. They say you can expect a

---

[4] Just so we're clear on this, a **meteor** is a rock that flames across the sky. A **meteorite** is a meteor that hits the ground before burning up. A **meteoroid** is a rock that hasn't reached the earth's atmosphere and so isn't burning yet.

[5] Or NL West, as the case may be.

meteor strike that would kill 100 people about once every 100,000 years.

If a giant meteorite does come our way, you definitely want more than an umbrella for protection. A meteorite one kilometer (about three-fifths of a mile) in diameter would gouge a crater 13 kilometers wide.

Some past meteorite strikes have been extremely destructive. One in northern Arizona about 50,000 years ago left a hole 600 feet deep and about four-fifths of a mile across. Chubb Crater in northern Quebec, now a lake, is about 2⅓ miles across. The largest crater of all may be on the eastern shore of Hudson Bay in Canada. It's an unbelievable 400 miles wide.

In recent times most serious meteorite strikes have consisted of rocks crashing through roofs and other small-time stuff. But there may have been a big one in 1908 in Siberia. Nobody is quite sure what happened, but a huge explosion one night destroyed all the trees in a five-mile circle. Some scientists believe the damage was caused by a meteorite that exploded in midair.

A giant meteorite could cause other, even worse kinds of damage. It might throw up a cloud of smoke and dust so huge it might block the sun, thus changing the weather for a time.

In fact, a few scientists think that's what killed off the dinosaurs 65 million years ago. They believe a giant meteorite six miles across struck the earth, filling the skies with dust. This caused the weather to become colder than the dinosaurs could stand and killed off many of the plants they fed on. Within a few years all the dinosaurs were dead. This theory hasn't been proven, but it gives you an idea of what could happen if a giant meteorite were to crash into the earth today.

Little meteorites are another story. They're usually harmless, and it's a good thing they are, because they hit the earth a lot more often—thousands of times a day, in fact. Most of them burn up in the air. But the dust that's left over does drift down to the ground eventually, anywhere from several dozen to several hundred tons' worth per *day*. That layer of dust on top of the stereo may just be garden dirt—but it *could* be trash from the depths of space.

IF SOMEBODY OPENED THE EMERGENCY EXIT ON AN AIRPLANE WHILE IT WAS IN THE AIR, WOULD EVERYBODY ON THE PLANE BE SUCKED OUT AND KILLED?

I used to wonder about this, too. My feeling was, a seat next to the emergency exit was not something you wanted to sell to a guy with a twitch, if you know what I mean. But no need to worry. He couldn't get that door open even if he wanted to.

The reason is that airplane doors don't open out, they open in. On the ground, which is where you're supposed to be when you use the emergency exit, that doesn't matter, because the air pressure is the same inside and out.

But up in the sky it's a different story. The air gets thinner the higher you go. At 30,000 feet—the typical **cruising altitude** (height) for a jet plane—the outside air pressure is only about 3 pounds per square inch. To keep everybody from dying for lack of oxygen, the crew **pressurizes** the cabin (fills it with air) to about 11 pounds per square inch.

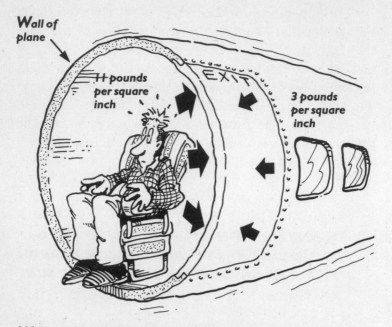

When a jet aircraft is flying at 30,000 feet, the inside (cabin) pressure is so much greater than the outside pressure that the emergency exit hatches are impossible to open.

So we've got 3 pounds pushing in, and 11 pounds pushing out. That gives us a net outward pressure of 8 pounds per square inch. (See illustration.) If the emergency exit has a total surface of 650 square inches, opening the door would be like lifting a 2½-ton weight. There's no way even Arnold Schwarzenegger could do it.

The same applies to the regular doors that you enter the plane through. True, they open out, but first they have to be yanked in a bit. So you wouldn't be able to get them open in flight either. Just as well. There are enough things to worry about on an airplane flight as it is.

IF A HELIUM BALLOON FLOATS AWAY, DOES IT DRIFT IN THE SKY FOREVER?

If it goes up, eventually it comes down.

Two things can happen to a helium balloon. First, the helium leaks out slowly, so that after rising for a while the balloon just drifts slowly back toward earth.

The second thing is actually far more likely. The balloon rises so high so fast that it pops. Remember, the higher you go, the lower the air pressure. The less *inward* pressure on the balloon, the more the helium inside presses *out*. So the higher the balloon floats, the bigger it gets. Eventually it stretches so much it breaks.

Some people want helium balloons to break when they get high in the air. The folks in the National Weather Service, for example. They send up weather balloons carrying special devices called **radiosondes** (RAY-dee-oh-sahnds), which measure temperature, air pressure, humidity, and so on.[6]

Radiosondes aren't cheap. The weather service wants the balloons to break eventually so the radiosondes will fall to the ground and people will return them to the government. Usually balloons pop when they reach 90,000 to 100,000 feet. A parachute then opens to slow the radiosonde's descent. Of course, most of the radiosondes

[6]We'll talk more about radiosondes on page 149.

probably wind up in trees or as souvenirs in somebody's garage. But you can't knock the government for trying.

IF I HELD ENOUGH HELIUM BALLOONS, COULD THEY CARRY ME AWAY?

You bet. But you wouldn't be the first.

One fellow who went up, up, and away was Larry Walters of California. Larry tied 42 weather balloons to an aluminum lawn chair. This turned out to be a couple balloons too many. When the rope that was holding him down broke, he shot 16,000 feet into the air.

Fortunately, he was ready. He had brought a pellet gun with him so he could shoot out balloons as needed to control his altitude. Being a thoughtful guy, he also brought a CB radio so he could warn passing airplanes.

Finally, after two hours in the air, he decided to land, so he shot out a few more balloons. The ones that were left pulled down some power lines on the way down, knocking out the electricity. But Larry himself escaped with nothing worse than a bad case of sunburn.

The government was not very happy with Larry. A safety inspector told the newspapers, "We know he broke some part of the Federal Aviation Act, and as soon as we decide which part it is, some type of charge will be filed."

Larry wound up paying a fine. On the plus side, he got to be on the David Letterman show. But he could easily have been killed. I don't want to lose any readers, so please don't try it yourself.

SPACE

6

IF YOU WERE THROWN INTO THE VACUUM OF SPACE WITHOUT A SPACE SUIT, WOULD YOU EXPLODE?

Naah.

Some folks—including some doctors—think otherwise. While they don't claim your body would blow up like a character in a science fiction movie, they do say the end might be pretty disgusting. Your eyeballs would explode. Your lungs would turn to pulp. Your blood would boil.

Well, your blood *would* boil. But that's not as bad as it sounds. It just means the blood would turn to vapor.[1] When the pressure returned to normal (normal for earth, that is), the blood would become liquid again. If this happened quickly enough, you'd recover without any permanent damage.

As for the rest of it—forget it.

Don't misunderstand me. You'd *die*, all right. But they wouldn't be sopping you up with a sponge. We know this because three Russian cosmonauts did die in the vacuum of space and their bodies didn't explode. (The air escaped from their space capsule after an accident.)

[1]Liquids can boil without becoming hot if the pressure of the atmosphere is low enough. Mountain climbers know that the higher they go, the thinner the air gets, and the lower the boiling point of water. In space water boils instantly.

In fact, you might even have 10 or 15 seconds before you blacked out. Time enough, perhaps, to save yourself. Or at least to think: "Boy, next time I read the *directions*."

How can the astronauts practice being weightless while still on the earth?

If you've ever watched videos of the astronauts bouncing around the cabin of their spacecraft while in orbit, you probably thought, this is a job I could learn to like. Well, there's no question it beats a newspaper route. But working in the weightlessness of space can take some getting used to. And naturally, we don't want our astronauts wasting a lot of valuable tax dollars practicing their moves while actually *in* space.

Luckily, the folks at NASA (the National Aeronautics and Space Administration) found they could re-create the feeling of weightlessness on earth using jet planes. First they sent the astronauts up in fighter jets to fly in a special pattern called a **parabolic** (par-uh-BAHL-ik) **arc.** (See illustration.) This pattern requires that the plane climb rapidly, then curve into a dive. When the astronaut is at the top of the curve, he or she is weightless for a short time.

If you've ever ridden a roller coaster, you've experienced the same thing. Have you ever noticed how, when the roller coaster levels off at the top of a hill, you're lifted up in your seat briefly, just before you plunge down the other side? That's because you have just enough upward speed to cancel out the force of gravity. For a split second, you're weightless.

Weightless
astronauts

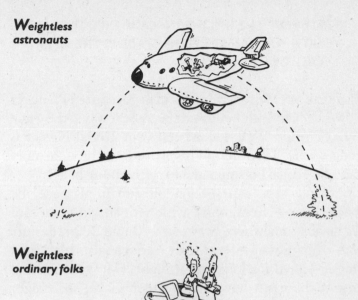

Weightless
ordinary folks

Later NASA sent the astronauts for another roller-coaster plane ride, only this time they were in the hold of a big cargo jet. NASA found that a pilot who knew what he was doing could make the weightlessness last 30 to 60 seconds. That's not long, but it's enough to give the astronauts a chance to practice eating, drinking, and performing other simple tasks in zero gravity.

By the way, most astronauts aren't too crazy about this part of their training. Their nickname for the roller-coaster plane is the "Vomit Comet."

Is it true the only man-made object on earth you can see from space is the Great Wall of China?

Of course not. Where this silly idea got started I'll never know, but everybody believes it because it was in the game Trivial Pursuit. Well, let me tell you: Trivial Pursuit is *wrong, wrong, WRONG!* (This attitude has brought more than one Trivial Pursuit game to a screaming halt.)

Actually, you can see *lots* of stuff from space. By "space" I mean "from orbit," which for an astronaut usually means somewhere between 100 and 200 miles up. From this distance you can see canals, highways, bridges—anything long and straight. (Most natural features of the earth have an irregular shape, so straight things stand out.)

Sometimes you can see even more. During the *Gemini* V mission, astronauts Gordon Cooper and Charles Conrad saw a rocket-sled test in New Mexico, a special checkerboard pattern that had been laid out for them in Texas, and two of the ships that were waiting for them in the Atlantic Ocean.

Some people say the Great Wall of China is the only thing you can see from the moon. That isn't true, either. According to the guys who've been there, all you can see on earth is white stuff (clouds and snow), blue stuff (water), yellow stuff (deserts), and brown and green stuff (vegetation). You can't make out any detail at all. If you don't believe me, go to the library and look at the pictures of earth taken during the lunar missions.

But some people never listen. A while back I saw an ad that said the Great Wall of China is the only man-made object you can see from *Mars*. And people wonder why I get grumpy.

HOW COME THE MOON IS BIGGER WHEN IT'S NEAR THE HORIZON THAN WHEN IT'S OVERHEAD?

It *isn't* bigger. Everybody just *thinks* it is. That's why this is called the "moon illusion."

To prove the moon illusion isn't real, here's a simple experiment. Just after moonrise, when the moon is near the horizon, go outside and measure it with a home-made **caliper** (KAL-uh-per—a device to measure widths). Make your caliper from a paper clip, as shown in the drawing. Then hold it at arm's length and bend the ends so they appear to touch the sides of the moon, also as shown.

By using a paper clip caliper to measure the moon at different times during the night, you can prove that the moon isn't bigger when it's near the horizon.

Now wait several hours, till the moon is overhead. Hold your paper-clip caliper at arm's length and measure the moon again. You'll find it's exactly the same size.

So why does the moon look bigger near the horizon? People have been arguing about that for 2,000 years. The simplest explanation is that the seeming difference in size is an illusion of **perspective.**

Perspective is a technique artists use to fool the eye into thinking a picture is three-dimensional rather than flat. But perspective can fool the eye in other ways as well.

Look at the drawing on the facing page. The circle near the top of the page looks small, right? Now look at the circle near the bottom of the page, above the drawing of the trees. Looks bigger, doesn't it? But it's the same size as the one on top.

Here's what happens. The circle at the top is dwarfed by the white expanse of the page, so it looks small, in much the same way the moon overhead looks small when surrounded by the vastness of the night sky.

In the bottom drawing, on the other hand, the march of objects toward the horizon makes the circle seem large. The march of objects to the horizon in real life makes a low-hanging moon seem larger, too.

Some people prefer a slightly different explanation. They say we think of the sky as being a flattened bowl. In other words, things directly overhead seem closer than those at the horizon. So when we see the moon at the horizon, we think to ourselves, "Gee, the moon is really far away. It must be really big." When the moon is directly overhead, though, we say, "Wow, the moon is pretty close. It must be smaller than I thought." This explanation doesn't do much for me, but if you like it, fine.

When the moon is overhead, the vastness
of the night sky makes it look small.

The march of objects to the horizon makes
the moon look larger.

How come the solar system is flat?

What's that? You didn't know the solar system *was* flat? Well, it is. If you were to look at the solar system from above (you can't really say "above" in space, but you know what I mean), it would look like this:

Top view of the solar system

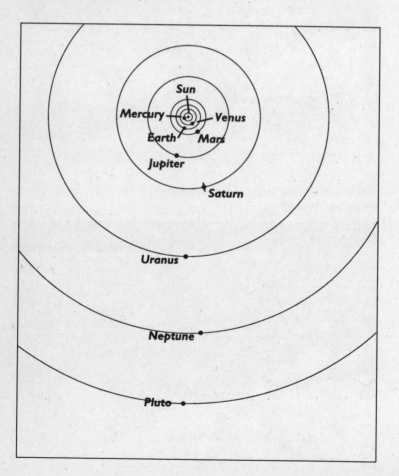

But if you looked at the solar system from the side, it would look like this:

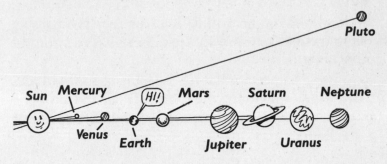

Side view of the solar system: It's flat!

In other words, the solar system is flat. (The only orbit that differs noticeably is Pluto's, which we'll talk about in a moment.)

That seems odd. Most times when things just hang in space, they're ball-shaped. A soap bubble, for instance. Or a planet.

Why is the solar system different? Because it's *spinning*. When objects spin, **centrifugal** (sen-TRIFF-a-gull) **force** causes them to fly outward.

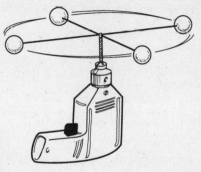

Here's why it's flat: Centrifugal force

Suppose you had a bunch of small rubber balls with string attached to them, and you tied them to an electric drill.[2]

Now turn on the drill. What happens? The balls fly out to the side, spinning in a flat disc. That's centrifugal force in action.[3]

The solar system is flat for the same reason, with the planets spinning around the center of it all, the sun.[4] The plane in which most of the orbits lie is called the **plane of the ecliptic.**

So what's the deal with Pluto?

Ah, yes. Most of the planets' orbits lie close to the plane of the ecliptic. But there's one exception—the ninth planet, Pluto.

Look again at the side view of the solar system on page 111. Pluto is tilted quite a bit, unlike the other planets. Its orbit is much narrower as well. Sometimes Pluto cuts inside the orbit of the planet next door, Neptune, and becomes the eighth planet.

---

[2]This is pretty cool to watch, but *don't* do it.
[3]Strictly speaking, centrifugal "force" is not a force, but I don't have the strength to go into it now.
[4]That raises another question: What got the planets orbiting around the sun in the first place? Mainly the fact that (1) the sun and planets were all made from a big ball of goo, and (2) billions of years ago that big ball was spinning. Why was it spinning? Never mind. But because of centrifugal force, the ball flattened out into a disc.
After a while some of the goo began to stick together and formed **proto-planets** (PROTE-o-plan-ets), the beginnings of new planets. The proto-planets got bigger and more solid until finally they formed full-fledged planets. (The biggest clump of stuck-together goo remained in the center to form the sun.) By that time, the planets weren't part of a disc of goo anymore, but their orbits still formed a disc.

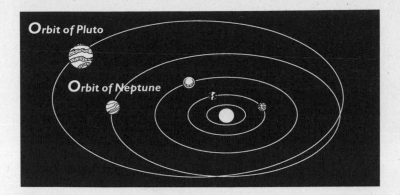

Sometimes (like now) Pluto cuts inside the orbit of Neptune, making Pluto the eighth planet rather than the ninth.

As a matter of fact, that's what's happening right now. Pluto has been the eighth planet since 1979, and it'll stay that way until 1999.

Astronomers aren't sure why Pluto acts differently from the rest of the planets. Some think Pluto's strange orbit shows it wasn't one of the original planets at all, but rather a moon of Neptune that broke loose somehow. Perhaps some giant unknown planet flew close by Neptune long ago and the force of its gravity pulled Pluto away. Nobody knows for sure.

Here's something else unusual. Most planets have moons with orbits that look something like the illustration on page 114.

The only exception is earth's moon, whose orbit lies very close to the plane of the ecliptic. What's more, our moon is much larger than planets the size of earth usually have.

What does this mean? Some scientists think the moon was once a full-fledged planet that was formed at the same time as the rest of the solar system. Long ago,

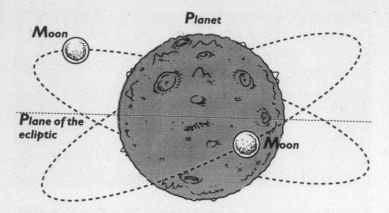

Most moons float around their planets any which way. But earth's moon (the Moon moon) lines up with "plane of the ecliptic." Some scientists think that's because the Moon was once a planet.

they believe, it crashed into the earth. What was left afterward bounced back into space and began to orbit around the earth. Dangerous place, this solar system. Be glad you're living now and not then.

HOW DO THE ASTRONAUTS GO TO THE BATH-ROOM IN SPACE?

No snickering here, folks; this is serious business. When you gotta go, you gotta go, even if you're an astronaut.

Consider the problem. In your regular earth toilet, the user (A) places him- or herself above the toilet (B). Waste gets from point A to point B by means of the miracle of gravity.

In space, you don't have gravity. Stuff just floats. You see the difficulty this presents. (I'm certainly not going to spell it out for you.) So scientists had to use a different way to get waste from point A to point B. What they came up with was a high-tech vacuum cleaner.

Here's how it works. The astronaut sits firmly on a special toilet seat. The seat makes a firm seal with the astronaut's skin, preventing anything from drifting off into the cabin.

Then he or she switches on a fan inside the toilet. This creates a gentle suction that pulls the waste into the toilet. The solid stuff collects in a special bag, while the wet stuff flows through the bag into a pipe and eventually gets pumped to a storage tank.

When the astronaut is done, he or she closes the top of the toilet tightly and opens a valve that permits the air inside the toilet to escape into the vacuum of space. This causes the moisture in the solids to boil away instantly. A special gizmo packs away what remains for disposal when the spacecraft gets back to the ground.

Great, you say. But what if, as so often happens in the space program, it doesn't work?

Well, there are several backup systems. If all else fails, there's always the "Apollo bag," so called because it was what the astronauts used on the Apollo flights. Basically, it's a plastic bag. You use it pretty much the way you'd figure you'd use it. Believe me, being an astronaut is a lot less glamorous than it's made out to be.

DOES THE FULL MOON REALLY MAKE PEOPLE ACT CRAZY?

A lot of people sure think it does. Police officers and emergency room nurses often say there are more crimes, more accidents, and more general craziness during the full moon than at any other time.

Well, with no disrespect to cops and nurses, I don't believe it—and most scientists back me up.

It's true that a few studies of the "moon effect" have claimed that the full moon does affect the way human beings act—that it makes them "loony."[5] But in most cases, it turns out those studies were wrong.

For example, one study found that an unusually large number of traffic accidents occurred during the full moon. But later it was learned that during the period being examined, an unusually large number of full moons fell on weekends. Traffic accidents are always higher on weekends because people are out whooping it up. When the figures were adjusted to account for this, the "moon effect" vanished.

But come on, you say. Everybody knows the moon causes ocean tides. Our bodies are mostly water, and we're a lot smaller than the oceans. Shouldn't the moon affect us, too?

The main problem with this reasoning is that the tides occur once or twice a day. So if there really were a moon effect, it should show up every day, not just during the full moon.

Which leads to an obvious question: What's so special about a full moon? Nothing much. A full moon occurs when the moon and the sun are lined up on opposite sides of the earth. (See illustration.)

Could it be that the sun is the real culprit behind the "moon effect"? Not really. Because the sun is so much far-

[5]"Lunacy," or craziness, comes from the Latin *luna*, moon.

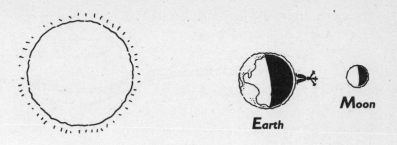

During the full moon, the moon and sun are lined up on opposite sides of the earth.

ther away from us, it tugs only half as hard on us as the moon does.

So are people just imagining things when they claim life is nuttier during the full moon? Not exactly. Mostly they're not thinking clearly. If the full moon is out and crazy things happen, they count that as evidence that the "moon effect" is real. But the truth is, crazy events are *always* happening. It's just that you don't attach any importance to them if they don't occur during a full moon.

WHY DO THE STARS TWINKLE?

For the same reason the air shimmies above a radiator or a fire or hot pavement: because of warm air rising in the atmosphere.

Heat can move in one of three ways. The first is **conductance** (kun-DUK-tenss). In conductance, the heat passes through something solid, such as wood or metal. (See illustration). This process is pretty slow.

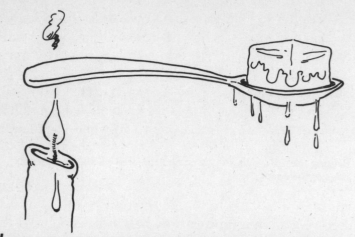

Heat transfer method #1 – Conductance. Heat travels through a solid material, such as metal.

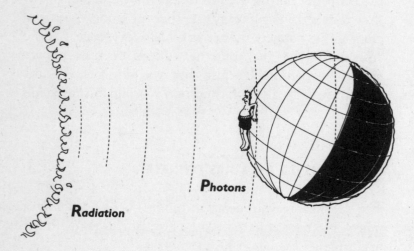

Heat transfer method #2 – Radiation. Heat is carried in the form of little energy packets called "photons."

Another way heat moves is **radiation.**[6] In radiation, the heat passes directly through space in the form of **photons** (FOE-tonns), tiny packets of energy traveling at the speed of light.

Radiation is the way the sun's warmth reaches earth. Sunlight travels 93 million miles in about eight minutes. Obviously, radiation is the way to go when you're on a tight schedule.

Finally, there's **convection.** In convection, heat warms the air. The warm air becomes less dense (and thus lighter) than the cool air around it, so it rises.[7] Convection is the reason the stars twinkle.

When air heated by convection rises, it tumbles and swirls. (Sort of like smoke rising out of a chimney, only it's

*H*eat transfer method #3—Convection. Heated air rises.

[6]Radiation does not have to mean *nuclear* radiation. There are two kinds of radiation: **ionizing** (EYE-uh-nigh-zing) and nonionizing. Right now we're talking about nonionizing radiation, which is the good kind.
[7]We talk about why hot air is lighter than cold air on pages 145-146.

invisible.) When light passes from the cool, dense air through the warm, swirling, not-so-dense stuff and back again, it gets bent this way and that. That's why the air shimmies over a fire or a radiator.

As air warmed by the earth rises through the atmosphere, it breaks into bubbles of warm air. As light from the stars passes through the bubbles, it's bent back and forth. This is what makes the stars seem to twinkle.

If there weren't any atmosphere, as on the moon, the stars would shine steadily. That would be great if you were an **astronomer** (uh-STRAHN-uh-mer—a star scientist), because the view through your telescope would be much clearer. But it'd be curtains for the song "Twinkle Twinkle Little Star."

7
FOOD AND DRINK

**WHEN A CEREAL SAYS "FORTIFIED WITH IRON,"
DOES THAT MEAN IT HAS PIECES OF METAL FLOAT-
ING AROUND IN IT?**

Yes.

You think I'm kidding, right? I'm not. If you were to
run a powerful magnet through some "fortified" breakfast
cereals, you'd find some tiny black specks sticking to it.
Those specks would be iron filings.

Are cereal makers playing some kind of weird joke on
us? Not at all. Your body needs iron—not as much as a
Chevy Camaro needs, but some. Eating iron filings is as
good a way as any of getting the iron you need into your
system. Bear in mind that these are very *small* iron filings.[1]
They aren't strong enough to set off an airport metal
detector, but they're iron just the same.

---

[1] Sometimes iron compounds (iron combined with other chemicals) are
used instead of pure iron.

Why do wintergreen Life Savers make little clouds of blue sparks when you crunch them with your teeth?

Sparking Life Savers are what is known as a phenomenon (feh-NOM-uh-non). A **phenomenon** is (1) an interesting event that (2) someone sees. It may seem a little stuffy when someone says "Observe the phenomenon," but you can't have famous scientists going around saying things like, "Yo, Elroy, check *this* out."

If you've never actually seen a sparking Life Saver, go out and get a package of the wintergreen kind quick. Avoid stale ones—they get soggy, which damps down the sparks. Next, find a pitch-dark room and an assistant, preferably cute. (You never know.) Have your assistant prop one Life Saver upright between his/her back molars while holding her/his mouth open.

Then have your assistant crunch with vigor. You'll see a tiny cloud of blue sparks. Quite a sight, but perfectly harmless.

What we have here is something called **triboluminescence** (try-bow-loo-mih-NESS-ents). Triboluminescence, or TL, is light resulting from crushing or tearing.

Now, you could probably get through life without knowing exactly how triboluminescence works. On the other hand, if you're stumped for conversation at a party some night, it might come in handy. So here's the TL story.

Step #1. When the sugar crystals in the Life Savers get crunched, **electrons** break loose and scoot all over creation. You know what electrons are, right? I see. Well, back to the basics. Check out the following illustration.

An atom

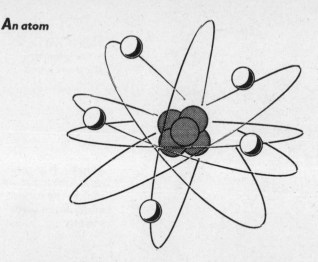

What we've got here is an **atom**, the basic building block of the universe.[2] The center of it is called the **nucleus** (NEW-klee-us). The electrons fly around the nucleus like little planets. But when the sugar is crushed, some break free.

Step #2. Meanwhile, heaps of **nitrogen molecules** (NIGH-truh-jen MOLL-uh-kyools) are floating around nearby. Nitrogen is an invisible gas that makes up four-fifths of the air around us. Nitrogen molecules are nothing more than clumps of nitrogen atoms. As the sugar crystals break, the nitrogen molecules stick to them at the places where the electrons broke free.

Step #3. The electrons begin to get lonesome for the sugar crystals they broke free from, and decide to return. However, since the nitrogen molecules are already there, the electrons end up crashing into the nitrogen.

---

[2] I was trying to work up a joke here about the original building blocks of the universe being "atom and Eve." However, I gave up. Count your blessings.

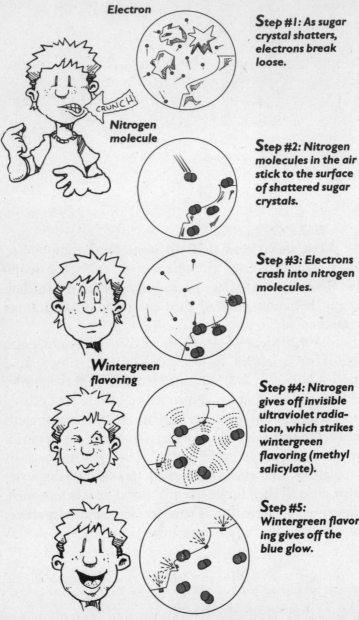

Electron

Step #1: As sugar crystal shatters, electrons break loose.

CRUNCH

Nitrogen molecule

Step #2: Nitrogen molecules in the air stick to the surface of shattered sugar crystals.

Step #3: Electrons crash into nitrogen molecules.

Wintergreen flavoring

Step #4: Nitrogen gives off invisible ultraviolet radiation, which strikes wintergreen flavoring (methyl salicylate).

Step #5: Wintergreen flavoring gives off the blue glow.

Step #4. The crashing electrons cause the nitrogen to emit **ultraviolet radiation**.

Note: THIS ISN'T NUCLEAR RADIATION. Ultraviolet radiation is a kind of light. Except for giving you sunburn (if there's a lot of it), it's harmless.

Step #5. The ultraviolet radiation then hits the wintergreen flavoring, called **methyl salicylate**.[3] This makes the flavoring glow with the bright blue light you see.

One last question may occur to you:

Is the fact that wintergreen Life Savers make clouds of sparks when crunched of any practical use?

No. On the other hand, if I was trapped in a pitch-dark cavern with no light source except a roll of wintergreen Life Savers, I'd sure give 'em a try.

How do they get the M's on M&Ms?

Tiny paintbrushes, maybe? Try a printing press. As I understand it (the folks at M&M company were a little cagey about this), the candies are fitted into little holes in a conveyor belt, and the belt is then run through the press.

The real trick, according to the M&M company, is adjusting the press so it doesn't smash the peanuts. Regular M&Ms, which are all the same size, are easy to print on. But the size of peanut M&Ms varies. If some peanuts get in that are too big, we're talking M&M-

---

[3] I don't know how to pronounce it, either.

flavored peanut butter. If the peanut M&Ms are too small, they don't get printed on at all.

Aᴿᴇ ᴀʟʟ ᴛʜᴇ ᴠɪᴛᴀᴍɪɴꜱ ɪɴ ᴀ ᴘᴏᴛᴀᴛᴏ ʀᴇᴀʟʟʏ ɪɴ ᴛʜᴇ ᴘᴇᴇʟ?

A simple enough question, but the answer is a little complicated.

Not all of a potato's vitamins are found in the peel; in most cases, the vitamins are spread pretty evenly throughout the potato. But eating the peel is still a good idea. Certain **minerals** that your body needs, such as calcium and zinc, are found in larger amounts in the peel.

The peel is also a good source of **fiber**. Fiber consists of things your body can't digest. As the fiber scrapes along your insides, it sops up bad stuff and carries it out of your body. Most of us could use a lot more fiber in our diets.

What's more, in baked potatoes, the peel *does* contain more than its share of vitamins. Baking causes vitamins and other nutrients to pile up in the peel.

So eating the peel sounds like a great idea, right? Well, it is, except for one thing: It also might poison you.

Here's the scoop. Potatoes are members of the nightshade family. The stems, seeds, and skins of this family are poisonous—some more so than others. In fact, you may have heard of a plant called **deadly nightshade**,[4] which can kill.

---

[4] It's got small white flowers, black berries, and triangular leaves. Other than that, it looks pretty much like any other plant. Watch what you eat.

Potatoes aren't as bad as deadly nightshade, but they're not completely harmless either. While the flesh of the potato (the white part) is okay, the leaves and skin contain substances called **glycoalkaloids** (GLY-ko-AL-ka-loids). Eat enough of these and you could get sick.

That's why you should never eat potato eyes—that's where the glycoalkaloids concentrate. If you come across some old potatoes that have sprouted (the eyes have begun to grow), throw them out immediately. Sprouted potatoes are loaded with glycoalkaloids, and are pretty rank in general.

The potatoes grown in this country have been carefully chosen for the low amount of glycoalkaloids in them, so you'd have to eat a *lot* of potato skins before you noticed any ill effects. Most potato scientists (there really are such people) think the benefit of the fiber and other good things in the peel outweighs the slight danger of poisoning. Still, it never hurts to be careful.

So WHAT ABOUT APPLE SKINS?

Apple skins you can (and should) eat without a second thought—assuming you've washed off any **pesticides** first. Apple skins are a good source of fiber, and there aren't any glycoalkaloids to worry about. If you eat an apple, peel and all, you get twice as much fiber as you do when you eat just the insides.

So, you think you'll skip the spuds and just eat apples the rest of your life? Don't be too hasty. Apple seeds contain the makings of **cyanide** (SIGH-uh-nide), a deadly poison. But there's no cause for alarm: you'd have to eat a cupful or more to suffer any ill effects.

How come some potato chips are green?

Another tale of horror from the fruit and vegetable front. Why they permit these deadly products to be sold without warning labels I'll never know.

Let's begin at the beginning. From time to time, you see two kinds of unusual potato chips. Number one are your brown potato chips. Brown chips are harmless. They come from potatoes that stayed in storage too long before they were made into chips. When that happens, too much sugar builds up in the potato. When the potato is cooked, the sugar turns brown. The potato chip may seem a little crunchy, but you won't double up in agony after eating it.

Green potato chips are something else again. They're the result of something called **sun scald**.

Potatoes usually grow underground, but sometimes one pokes above the surface and is exposed to the sun. The sun turns it green inside. The green is **chlorophyll** (KLORE-ah-fill), the chemical found in all green plants.

Chlorophyll itself won't hurt you. But at the same time the sun makes chlorophyll, it also makes another chemical called **solanine** (SO-la-neen). Solanine is one of the glycoalkaloids we talked about in the last question. Eating a green potato is just like eating potato eyes or potato leaves.

Now, how many green potato chips would you have to

eat to actually *die?* Untold millions. So maybe green potato chip poisoning doesn't rank up there with nuclear war
on the list of major health threats. But there's no sense in
taking chances.

How come ketchup bottles are tall and skinny and mustard bottles are short and fat?

What do you mean, who cares? What kind of attitude is
that? If it weren't for humanity's restless curiosity, we'd
still be living in trees eating bananas. Worse, nobody
would buy this book.

We'll work this out scientifically. How do you put
ketchup on food? You pour it straight out of the bottle.
That's because ketchup isn't very spicy and you can use a
lot of it. For pouring, a narrow spout is best.

Mustard is different. Mustard has such a sharp taste
you only need a small amount of it. So you use a knife,
which you can handle better when the mouth of the jar is
wide. And if the jar is short and squat, it won't tip over
when you poke your knife in it.

In restaurants the situation is a little different. They
don't want you poking your grubby silverware into things.
So they use tall, skinny mustard bottles with narrow
mouths, just like ketchup bottles. It requires you to pour
the mustard the same way you do with ketchup. Sure, you
might pour too much and end up setting your insides afire.
But at least the next customer to come along won't have
to look at the crud *you* got in the mustard jar.

How come drinking water doesn't help when you're trying to cool off your mouth after eating spicy food?

We're dealing here with one of the world's basic truths: oil and water don't mix. The spices in most "hot" foods are oily. If you try to wash them away with water, the water just rolls off, leaving the oil behind. Fortunately, generations of suffering restaurant customers have worked out several remedies that will work.

One method is to eat bread. The bread absorbs the oil and carries it away. (Make sure you roll the bread around in your mouth a bit before swallowing to sop up as much oil as you can.)

Another solution is to try milk. A substance in the milk called **casein** (KAY-seen) acts like a detergent, combining with the oil and washing it away.

If things are really desperate, adults sometimes try the Tequila Alternative. Tequila is a Mexican liquor that dissolves the oil. (So does any form of alcohol.) Trouble is, it often means exchanging one problem for another—tequila makes many people feel terrible the next morning. I don't advise it.

Is it true that if you swallow chewing gum, it'll stay in your stomach for seven years?

No. It's true that chewing gum can't be digested, but that doesn't mean it hangs around in your stomach. Basically, it goes in one end of you and out the other at the same time as everything else.

How come I can swallow when I'm upside down? Why doesn't the stuff just fall out?

This is the big difference between us and chickens.[5] Chickens *can't* swallow when they're upside down. To take a drink, they have to grab a mouthful, then point their mouths toward the sky so the water will go down their throats by force of gravity.

That's because chickens haven't got the remarkable throat muscles we've got. When we swallow, our throat muscles make a series of wavelike movements called **peristalsis** (pare-uh-STALL-sis).

Here's how peristalsis works. Suppose you had a rubber ball inside a sock. And suppose the ball were too big to slip through the sock easily. How could you move the ball along? Simple: Just grab the sock and push the ball from behind, as shown in the illustration.

Swallowing works the same way, only it's the muscles in your throat that do the pushing. The process works so well that you can even drink water upside down: your throat muscles are able to push it up to your stomach like a little elevator.

Peristalsis continues working even after the food leaves your stomach and moves into your **intestines** (in-

[5]OK, not the *only* difference.

Just as you can shove a ball through a sock by shoving behind it, the muscles in your throat push food into your stomach—even if you're upside down.

TESS-tinz—your guts, to be blunt), where the food is broken down and digested. The wavelike movements of the intestine muscles move the food along until it leaves by the back door.

IS IT TRUE THAT IF YOU ATE NOTHING BUT CARROTS YOU WOULD TURN ORANGE?

Sure is. If you really got carried away you might even die, and boy, would you make a strange-looking corpse. But death from carrot poisoning is pretty rare—probably about as rare as green potato chip poisoning.[6]

[6]Either way, I would definitely want to go to the wake.

Carrots contain an orange **pigment**, or coloring, called **carotene** (CARE-uh-teen). Eat enough of them (try bushels), and you could get **carotenosis** (CARE-uh-teh-NO-sis), in which the skin turns orange.

Don't let this talk of carrot overdoses scare you, though. Carotene in normal amounts is good for you. Some scientists believe it even helps prevent cancer. In addition to carrots, carotene can be found in cantaloupe, squash, and broccoli. Why isn't the good stuff ever in hot dogs or Chicken McNuggets? That's a question even I can't answer.

WHY DO SO MANY FOOD PACKAGES SAY "REG. PENNA. DEPT. AGR." ON THEM?

It's 7:30 A.M. and you're sitting at the breakfast table reading the back of the doughnut box. In small type at the bottom you notice the mysterious words, "Reg. Penna. Dept. Agr."

Hey, you think, I've seen this before. And indeed you have. "Reg. Penna. Dept. Agr." turns up on all sorts of baked goods. It means "Registered with the Pennsylvania Department of Agriculture." But that merely raises another question: Where does the Pennsylvania Department of Agriculture get off registering my food?

(We're assuming here that you don't live in Pennsylvania. If you do, you probably think it's perfectly natural that the Penna. D. of A. registers things. But think how the rest of us feel.)

It all goes back to the Pennsylvania Bakery Law of 1933. Baked goods made in factories were just then beginning to be sold in stores. Previously, baked goods had been made either at home or in local bakeries.

Pennsylvanians worried that factory-made goods might not be as carefully made as Mom's. So they passed stiff rules saying that all baked goods sold in Pennsylvania had to pass certain standards for cleanliness and honest weight.

But the big food company factories sent baked goods all over the country. The companies couldn't be sure which of their products would go to Pennsylvania and which wouldn't. Not wanting to take chances, they had all their factories inspected, just in case. That way they could truthfully mark all of their packaging "Reg. Penna. Dept. Agr.," even though many of the products didn't get anywhere near the Keystone State. That makes it easier for them, slightly confusing for the rest of us.

WHAT DOES IT MEAN WHEN A FOOD PACKAGE SAYS "100 PERCENT NATURAL" ON IT?

Nothing at all.

People *think* it means something, though, and the food companies know it. So they cheerfully put "100 percent natural" and "all natural" on their products to convince you they're somehow better for you, even though they may contain all sorts of preservatives and other "unnatural" ingredients.

How do they get away with it? It's our own fault. The

sad fact is, nobody can agree on what "natural" should mean.

For example, a lot of people think "natural" should mean that a product doesn't contain refined sugar (the white stuff you find in the sugar bowl). When we eat too much sugar, we get fat and our teeth rot.

But there's no way you can say sugar is an "unnatural" product. It comes from sugar cane or sugar beets, plants that are grown on large farms. These plants are then crushed, and the sugary juice is removed from them, in much the same way that orange juice or apple juice is made.

The sugary juice is dried and packaged and eventually winds up on your table, or in your cupcakes, or whatever. Too much of it may not be good for you, but that doesn't mean it's not natural.

Other words often seen on packages don't mean much, either—or at least they didn't use to. For example, often you'd see the word "light" or "lite." You might have thought a "lite" product would have fewer calories or perhaps less fat or sugar. But you would have been wrong. Sometimes a company would use "light" just to mean that the product was lighter in color. Pretty funny, eh?

The government didn't think so, either. In fact, it once sued a big baked goods company over just that point. The company sold something it called "light classic" cheesecake. The ads gave the impression the cheesecake had fewer calories than regular cheesecake. It didn't. The company finally agreed not to call anything "light" unless it had one-third fewer calories than the regular kind. New government rules now prohibit anyone from trying this trick again.

WHAT DO THOSE LETTERS K, U, AND R ON FOOD LABELS MEAN?

Usually K and U mean that the product is kosher, that is, it complies with the Jewish dietary laws, which say that meat and milk products can't be mixed. Orthodox Jews, who are strict, take this very seriously, and even the slightest amount of milk in a meat product can contaminate the whole batch. So they're always on the lookout for kosher products.[7]

To have their products officially declared kosher, the food companies must hire a kosher inspection service, which sends out one or more rabbis[8] to inspect the plant. If everything is okay, the kosher inspection service will allow its mark to be put on the goods. K and U with circles around them are the marks of two of the bigger kosher inspection services.

Sometimes a food company may decide it doesn't want to pay to have the kosher inspection service come out. The boss may stroll through the plant, say, "Hey, looks kosher to me," and figure he's entitled to put an ordinary letter K on his packaging. And he is. While he's at it, he can also throw in Z, X, and Q. But without the circle around it, the K doesn't mean a thing.

The circled letter R that follows a name of a product means that the name is a registered trademark. When a name is trademarked, other companies aren't allowed to use it.

[7]The word "pareve" (PAR-eh-veh), which is sometimes next to the circled K or U, is a Yiddish word meaning the product was made without milk or meat products and so may be eaten with either. Yiddish is the language many Jews spoke in Europe.
[8]Jewish clergy. I know, I shouldn't have to explain this. But some people lead sheltered lives.

IS IT TRUE YOU CAN ONLY STAND EGGS ON END ONE DAY OUT OF THE YEAR?

According to legend, the one day a year you can stand eggs on end is March 21, the first day of spring, also known as the **vernal equinox** (EE-kweh-nox). On the vernal equinox, day and night are the same length, and the sun passes directly over the earth's equator. A few folks got the idea this meant the force of gravity was put in balance somehow, making it easier to balance eggs.

Well, here's a news flash: You can stand eggs on end *any old time*, not just on the vernal equinox. All you need are steady hands and a lot of patience. Also, it wouldn't hurt to have about a dozen eggs. (Some are flatter on the bottom than others.) My method is to concentrate, try real hard, and if at first you don't succeed, give up. No sense killing yourself over a stupid egg. Besides, the next one in the box may be easier.

It helps if you shake the egg up first, by the way. That breaks loose the yolk. Normally, the yolk hangs in the center of the egg from two bands called **chalazae** (kuh-

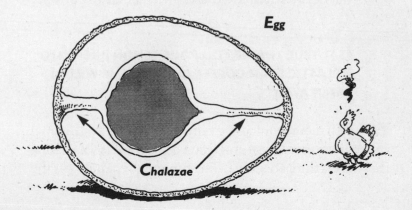

Egg

Chalazae

LAY-zee). (They're the white stringy things you sometimes see attached to the yolk when you break the egg—
see the illustration.)

Break the chalazae and the yolk sinks to the bottom.
That makes the egg bottom heavy and easier to stand up.

It's also cheating. But if the audience is waiting and
your reputation is on the line . . . well, let your conscience
be your guide.

SUPPOSE I WANT TO MAKE JUST ONE SLICE OF TOAST, BUT INSTEAD OF PUTTING THE BREAD IN THE TOASTER SLOT MARKED "ONE SLICE," I USE THE OTHER SLOT. WHAT WILL HAPPEN? WILL THE TOASTER EXPLODE?

Don't be silly. You won't wreck the toaster, but you might
get burned (or underdone) toast. The toaster's **thermostat**, the thing that measures how hot the toast is, is in or
near the "one slice" slot. If you turn the toaster on and
there's no bread for the thermostat to measure, you take
your chances on when the toaster will decide to pop up.

IS IT TRUE THAT IF YOU POUR LEMON JUICE INTO A PLASTIC FOAM COFFEE CUP, THE CUP WILL BE EATEN AWAY?

You got it. Lemon juice contains a **solvent** (SAHL-vent)
called **limonene** (LIM-uh-neen). A solvent is something
that makes things dissolve. The limonene eats away at the

plastic foam. If there's enough of it, it may actually eat a hole in the cup.

The plastic foam turns into white crud that floats on the surface of the lemon juice. Years ago some scientists thought that if you weren't paying attention and drank the floating stuff, you might get cancer. But the companies that make plastic foam cups say *their* research shows you *won't* get cancer. (Big surprise, huh?) You'll just have to decide for yourself.

WHY DOES WATER HEATED IN A MICROWAVE OVEN FIZZ LIKE MAD WHEN YOU DUMP POWDER INTO IT?

Here's a little trick that can produce outstanding results if used with timing and skill.

Say you have this older brother who treats you like slime. Sunday morning he comes staggering down to the breakfast table after a rough night. Gazing cheerfully into his bloodshot eyes, you offer to make him a cup of instant coffee. He'll be so surprised he'll probably let you.

Put a cup of water into the microwave oven and zap it for three minutes. (You may have to experiment with the time for best results.) The water will become very hot, but it won't boil. Carefully place the cup of hot water in front of your brother, along with the instant coffee and a spoon. Now find some place where you can watch but still make a quick getaway.

Your brother dumps a heaping teaspoon of instant coffee into the hot water. For a second, nothing happens.

Then suddenly the water boils up like somebody just poured two quarts of toxic waste into it. (It might even boil over the side, so be careful.)

With luck, your brother will totally freak and figure you're trying to poison him. If he's the excitable type, he'll jump up, knock over the chair, trip over the table leg trying to chase after you, and in general make a complete idiot out of himself. You'll find this goes a long way toward making up for whatever abuse he's given you over the years.

In case you're wondering, the coffee is perfectly safe to drink. The fizzing is caused by a phenomenon called **superheating**. Here's how it works.

When you boil water on an ordinary gas or electric stove, the water at the bottom of the container, which is closest to the heat, gets hot first. Because of *convection*, which we talked about on pages 117-120, the hot water becomes less dense and begins to rise. Meanwhile the cool water on top begins to sink. The result is that you get *convection currents*. (See illustration.)

Convection currents are what cause the churning in the water you see during a "rolling boil."

Things work differently when you heat up water in a microwave oven. The water doesn't get hot at the bottom first. Instead, it warms up evenly all over. That means no convection currents. The water doesn't move but instead remains very still.

Why does that matter? Because of an interesting fact about boiling: It doesn't just happen; it needs what we might call *seeds*.

If you ever boil water in a glass pot, you'll notice bubbles streaming from certain points (actually, tiny scratch-

**Convection currents.
Warm water rises, cold
water sinks.**

es) on the sides and bottom. These bubbles contain
steam. The scratches act as "seeds" for the bubbles—that
is, they give them a place to get started until they're big
enough to survive on their own. Scientists call these seed-
ing spots **nucleation** (new-klee-A-shun) **sites**.

On an ordinary stove, convection currents keep the
water constantly in motion. Eventually almost all the
water in the pot flows past the scratches on the bottom
and gets a chance to boil.

But in a microwave oven, the water stays perfectly
still. Most of it never gets close enough to the tiny scratches for bubbles to form. So the water never boils. In fact, it
actually may rise to several degrees *above* the boiling
point. That's superheating.

When you take the superheated water out of the
microwave and pour in instant coffee, what happens? You
provide thousands of "seeds." In seconds, the water boils.
Don't try explaining this to your brother. I'm not sure he'll
appreciate it.

Do YOU KNOW ANY AMAZING SCIENCE STUNTS THAT WOULD SHOW THE WONDER OF AIR PRESSURE AND AT THE SAME TIME CAUSE MASSIVE DESTRUCTION OF INNOCENT SODA CANS?

I thought you'd never ask. I have just the thing.

The purpose of this experiment is to show how much water expands when you boil it. First, get an empty aluminum soda can. Then get a small bowl or pie tin and fill it a half-inch deep with water. Finally, go find a responsible adult to watch you, so your parents won't sue me in case you accidentally burn down the house doing this.

Now put a small amount of water in the bottom of the aluminum can—maybe a quarter of an inch. Using protective gloves and a pair of long tongs (*not* your bare hands), hold the can over a hot burner on the stove until the water boils. (In all seriousness, be careful doing this so

Water   **Steam filling can**

you don't burn yourself.) Then quickly take the can off the burner and turn it upside down in the pie tin full of water, as shown.

If you do this right, the can will be suddenly crushed. Cool, eh? But why? Let's take this step by step.

First we boiled the water. When water turns to steam, it takes up more than 1,500 times[9] as much space. Originally, you only had a quarter inch of water in the can, but once it boiled, the steam filled the whole can and then some. (See illustration.)

When you turned the can upside down in the pie tin full of water, the water caused the steam to cool and turn back into liquid. When this happens, we say the steam has **condensed**. Naturally, the water took up only 1/1,500th

[9]At least I *think* it's 1,500 times. However, every time my brother-in-law with the Ph.D. works this one out, he comes up with a different number.

Steam fills can. Inside and outside pressure are equal.

Steam condenses. Inside pressure drops.

Can collapses.

as much space as the steam did. Normally air would have rushed into the can to fill the space where the steam had been. But since the can was upside down in water, the outside air couldn't get in.

What we got instead was what we call a **vacuum** (VAK-yewm). A vacuum is what you have in outer space—no air, no anything, just empty space.

A vacuum has a pressure of zero. So you have air on the outside of the can pressing in, but nothing on the inside pressing out.[10] The sides of the can are too weak to resist the strain, so they collapse. (See illustration.)

So there you have it. Now you can smash cans for the rest of the afternoon, knowing you are helping to advance the cause of knowledge. Ain't science great?

[10]To be honest, there's probably *some* pressure inside the can, but it's much less than the outside air.

THE WEATHER

WHY DOES THE WIND BLOW?

Because the sun shines, of course. Seems perfectly obvious to me. But I suppose if it were perfectly obvious to you, you wouldn't have bought this book.

The wind blows because the sun warms up some parts of the air more than others, and the warm air moves. This process is called **convection,** which we've talked about before.

To see convection in action, get yourself a candle and light it. (Make sure a responsible adult watches while you do this.[1]) Put your hand above the flame—*way* above the flame, silly. You can feel the heat rising, right? That's convection.

Warm air rises because it's *less dense* than cool air. It's less dense because heat makes the air molecules fly around pretty fast and they get far apart. The fewer air molecules you have per cubic inch, the less the air weighs. (See illustration.) So warm air will rise above cool air.

When the warm air rises, cool air rushes in to replace it. To see how this works, get a fat tin can with the top cut off. Turn the can over and punch two holes opposite one another on the bottom with a can opener.

[1]They're making me say this.

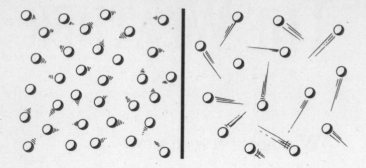

Cool air molecules move slowly, are packed close together. Warm air molecules move quickly, fly far apart. This makes warm air less dense than cool air.

Place the can over the lighted candle so the flame is directly beneath one of the holes. Then get another lighted candle and hold it near the other hole. (See illustration.) See what happens?

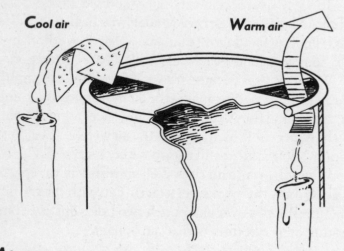

Cool air   Warm air

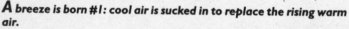

A breeze is born #1: cool air is sucked in to replace the rising warm air.

The flame is drawn toward the hole. Why? Because cool air is being sucked in to replace the warm air rising above the candle inside the can. In other words, the heat has created a tiny breeze.

Something similar happens when the sun warms the earth. The place on earth where the air gets hottest is around the equator, in the tropics. The warm tropical air rises, causing cooler air to blow in from the north and south.

As the warm tropical air drifts toward the North and South poles, it cools off and sinks back to earth's surface. Eventually the air drifts down to the tropics and the cycle repeats itself. (See illustration.)

A *breeze is born #2: warm air rises over the equator. Cool air is pulled in from the north and south to replace it.*

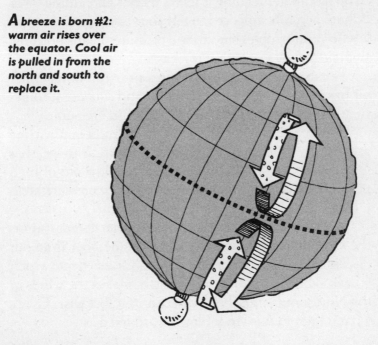

This constantly moving air is what we call the wind. To be sure, I'm making it all seem much simpler than it really is. (For one thing, I haven't explained why the wind changes direction—we'll tackle that next.) But when you get right down to it, what makes the wind blow is the sun's warmth.

How do they predict the weather?

TV weather forecasters often mention the **barometric** (bare-oh-MET-rik) **pressure.** For example, they may say, "The barometer reading is 29.82 inches and falling"—as if that's actually supposed to tell you something.

To most people, barometric pressure means nothing. But it's the key to weather forecasting.

A barometer measures air pressure. You don't think air has pressure? Blow up a balloon and squeeze it sometime. You feel resistance, right? That's air pressure.

The air pressure is higher in some parts of our swirling atmosphere than in others. That's important in weather forecasting because the winds tend to blow *out* of high pressure areas ("highs") and *in* toward low pressure areas ("lows").

Another important factor in weather forecasting is the **Coriolis effect,** which you may remember from our discussion of bathtub drains. The Coriolis effect, which is caused by the rotation of the earth, makes the winds in the Northern Hemisphere spin counterclockwise. Here's what it does to the winds blowing around a low:

Winds spiral toward a low in a counterclockwise direction.

So if you know where the highs and lows are, you know what direction the wind will be blowing. That in turn will give you a good idea what the weather will be like: a wind from the south will be warm, while a wind from the north will be cold.

To find out where the highs and the lows are, the National Weather Service sends up special measuring devices called **radiosondes** in helium balloons all over the country. (We talked about radiosondes on page 101.)

Radiosondes measure air pressure, temperature, and humidity, and send this information back to the ground via radio. By tracking what direction the balloons go, the weather service can also determine wind speed and direction.

Using the information from the radiosondes, meteorologists are able to draw weather maps showing the location of high- and low-pressure areas. You've probably seen these in the newspaper.

Highs and lows tend to move across the country from west to east because of the rotation of the earth. By charting the movement of highs and lows from one day to the next, meteorologists can estimate where these areas will be in the days ahead.

Once they've done that, they can predict wind direction, and once they've done *that*, they can estimate the temperature and whether it'll be stormy or not.

I STILL DON'T GET IT. WHY DO THEY BOTHER TELLING ME THE BAROMETRIC PRESSURE ON THE WEATHER REPORT IF I NEED ALL SORTS OF COMPLICATED EQUIPMENT TO PREDICT WHAT THE WEATHER WILL BE?

Because there's a shortcut.

Lows tend to produce cloudy weather, while highs produce clear weather. Why? Remember that air rushes in toward the center of a low. Where does it go when it gets there? The only place it can go—straight up.

The higher you get in the atmosphere, the cooler it gets. Cooling causes the moisture in the rising air to **condense**—that is, to change from vapor to water droplets. The water droplets form clouds. If you've got clouds, you can have rain. That's why lows are often linked to storms.

The opposite happens in a high. Air rushes out from the center of a high. Where does the air come from? From above, of course. As the air descends, it grows warmer, and the moisture in it turns from droplets into invisible vapor. So clouds disappear and the weather is fair.

So here's the shortcut: If the barometer reading is *above* 30 and *rising*, the weather will be clear and the winds will be light. If it's *below* 30 and *falling*, the weather will be cloudy, windy, and possibly stormy. If the barometer is above 30 and falling, or below 30 and rising, the weather is less predictable. If the barometer is steady, the weather will (surprise!) keep on doing whatever it's doing now.

WHAT IF I DON'T HAVE A BAROMETER?

No problem. A cup of coffee will do just fine. If the bubbles in the coffee float toward the rim of the cup, that means the pressure is low—look for clouds and stormy

When air pressure is high, the surface of the coffee is forced down and bubbles float toward the center of the cup.

When air pressure is low, the surface of the coffee bulges upward and bubbles float toward the rim.

weather. If the bubbles float toward the center of the cup, that means the pressure is high—which means fair weather.

Why does this work? Because high pressure forces the surface of the coffee down, and low pressure allows it to spring up. The bubbles always float to the lowest point on the surface of the coffee, as the illustration shows.

WHEN YOU'RE SHOVELING SNOW, WHY DOES THE METAL PART OF THE SHOVEL ALWAYS SEEM COLDER THAN THE WOOD PART?

Hint #1: See the answer to the question on pages 117-120. Hint #2: It's not convection or radiation. Bingo! It's conductance. Metal is a much more efficient **conductor** (kun-DUK-ter) of heat than wood is. In other words, heat is carried away from your hand much more rapidly by metal than by wood, so you feel the cold quicker. Now you know why they never make toilet seats out of steel.

IS IT TRUE IF YOU TOUCHED YOUR TONGUE TO A METAL FLAGPOLE IN THE MIDDLE OF WINTER IT WOULD STICK?

It sure would—and I'm sure the poor saps who took this dare in the fourth grade can back me up from personal experience. A similar thing happens when you grab a metal ice cube tray fresh out of the freezer—your hand sticks. (That's why most ice cube trays these days are made of plastic.)

What happens is that the thin layer of moisture that is always on your tongue (or your fingers, for that matter) freezes instantly to the metal. Remember, metal is a good conductor. It carries away heat very rapidly, so that the temperature of whatever is touching the metal drops quickly.

So don't go licking flagpoles, or you'll know what they'll call you for the rest of your life: tasteless.

IS IT TRUE NO TWO SNOWFLAKES ARE EVER ALIKE?

No. It's just that the chances of *finding* identical snowflakes are pretty slim, and scientists have better things to do than sit around all day comparing snowflakes.

Still, sometimes miracles happen. A scientist who was browsing around in some snow recently did find two identical snowflakes—or, to be exact, two identical snow *crystals*. They weren't the delicate six-sided flakes you see pictures of, but rather what looked like tiny six-sided pillars. But it was close enough for me.

HOW COME SNOW ON THE GROUND GRADUALLY DISAPPEARS EVEN IF THE TEMPERATURE STAYS BELOW FREEZING?

Sometimes in winter it stays below freezing for weeks at a stretch. But even though it never gets warm enough during that time for the snow to melt, the amount of snow gradually shrinks (assuming, of course, that more snow doesn't fall). How come?

It turns out the snow evaporates—that is, it turns directly into vapor. You probably thought this only happened with water. You know—you put a bowl of water out on the kitchen counter overnight, and the next morning it's all (or mostly) gone. Well, the same thing can happen with snow or ice.[2] There's even a name for it: **sublimation** (sub-lih-MAY-shun).

Water and ice evaporate because water molecules are lacking in the social graces, so to speak. If you could look at some water under a powerful microscope, you'd see the molecules were all jostling one another, like people on a crowded bus. (See illustration.)

Every once in a while the jostling gets so intense that a molecule gets thrown out of the bus altogether—in

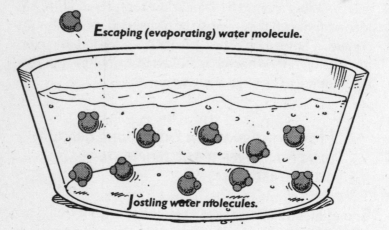

Escaping (evaporating) water molecule.

Jostling water molecules.

[2]Or chocolate chip cookies. Just in case you need a scientific explanation next time this happens.

other words, it escapes into the atmosphere.[3] As time goes on, the amount of water shrinks noticeably. That's evaporation in action.

The amount of jostling that goes on increases as the water gets hotter. That's because heat is a form of energy. The more energy, the more jostling. It's like feeding the molecules raw meat.

In ice, there's less heat, which means less energy, which means less jostling. But things are never completely quiet. As long as there's any activity at all, somebody's eventually going to get tossed out of the bus (or the snowdrift or the icicle), and the snow (or ice) is going to evaporate. It'll just take longer.

Is THERE A COLDEST POSSIBLE TEMPERATURE? OR, FOR THAT MATTER, A HOTTEST?

Yes to both questions. The coldest possible temperature is −460 degrees Fahrenheit. The hottest possible temperature is something called the **Planck temperature,** which we'll talk about in a moment.

The idea that there are limits to temperature may be hard to swallow. How can there be a coldest or hottest temperature? Can't you just add a few more ice cubes or throw a few logs on the fire to make it colder or hotter still?

No. When something is hot—say, a cup of water—its

---

[3]My editor prefers to think of the molecules as fish trying to escape from a net—every once in a while, one manages to flip out and escape.

molecules are vibrating (moving) very fast. As the water gets colder, its molecules slow down. Eventually the water (now ice) gets so cold the molecules don't move at all. That's absolute zero.

Heading in the opposite direction, things can get pretty toasty. But once you get to 10^{32} degrees Kelvin (that's 1 followed by 32 zeros), you've reached the Planck temperature. Many scientists say that's as hot as it can get—beyond that point, space and time lose all meaning.

So next time you're suffering through a heat wave, take comfort: things could be a lot worse.

How on earth did they come up with the Fahrenheit temperature scale? Why is freezing 32 degrees and boiling 212?

What was going through this guy Fahrenheit's head when he invented his scale, anyway? Why should freezing be 32? Why not 30? For that matter, why should boiling be 212? Was that his area code? Why couldn't Fahrenheit be like that nice Mr. Celsius, who made freezing 0 degrees and boiling 100, which are a lot easier to remember? (See illustration.)

Well... later I'm going to have to tell you a little story about Mr. Celsius. But first let's deal with Fahrenheit. Daniel Gabriel Fahrenheit, who lived in Holland from 1686 to 1736, was the first person to devise a practical thermometer using mercury inside glass. You may not think this is such a big deal, but before Fahrenheit came along, people had no way of knowing exactly how cold it

was outside. Conversations such as the following were common:

FRITZ: "Zo, Hans, it's kolt, yah?"

HANS: "It's *durn* kolt, Fritz."

FRITZ: "Hah, *yisterday* vas durn kolt. Today it's *pretty dadblastit fershlooginer* kolt."

HANS: "Nein, last *veek* it vas pretty dadblastit fershlooginer kolt. Today it's yust durn kolt."

FRITZ: "Yo' mama."

You see the problem. What was needed was a scale that everybody could agree on. Dan based his on that of Ole Romer, a Danish astronomer.[4] Romer had devised a scale that had 60 as the boiling point of water, 22½ as the

---

[4]No relation to Ole Yeller.

temperature of the human body, and 7½ as freezing.

Ole's system was okay except for the fractions. To get rid of them Dan multiplied Ole's degrees by 4. That gave him 30 for the freezing point of water (4 x 7½) and 90 for the temperature of the human body (4 x 22½). He skipped boiling point for the time being.

Thirty degrees for freezing wouldn't have been so bad, but Dan didn't know when to quit. For unknown reasons, he decided to multiply all of his numbers by ¹⁶/₁₅. This gave him 32 for the freezing point and 96 for body temperature.[5] Later he figured out that boiling point was 212 degrees.

The only problem was that 96 *wasn't* body temperature. When more exact measurements were done, it was discovered that body temperature was 98.6 degrees Fahrenheit.

The Celsius scale makes more sense. But its inventor was a bit of a goofball, too. When Anders Celsius first thought up his scale, he made *freezing* 100 degrees and *boiling* 0 degrees. In other words, he had the scale *upside down*. No one had the nerve to tell him this, though, so the other scientists waited until he died to change it.

Today the Celsius scale is used throughout much of the world, except (of course) in the United States, where we still use the Fahrenheit system. Why we got stuck with this loser system of measurement I'll never know.

---

[5]Some books say Dan was trying to get 100 degrees to be body temperature. Pay no attention to these books. I know what I'm talking about.

How can you tell if a tornado is coming?

First recommendation: Look out the window.

Second recommendation: Find a TV set. Tune to Channel 13. Turn the brightness control down until the picture is almost—but not completely—black. Then tune to Channel 2.

Lightning bolts will show up as flashes on the screen—no big deal. But when the picture suddenly becomes bright enough to be seen, or the screen glows with an even light, it's time to get out of there. Tornadoes create electrical interference at the same frequency as Channel 2. When the picture gets suddenly brighter, it means there's a twister within 20 miles.

What does the weather report mean when it says there's a "10 percent chance of showers"?

Exactly what it says. Over the years weather experts have learned to predict temperature, cloudiness, and wind speed and direction with good accuracy. But predicting rain or snow remains a hit-and-miss business. The best anybody can do is give you odds.

To figure the odds accurately, the weather bureau compares today's conditions with those in years past using information stored in computers. When the weather report says there is a "10 percent chance of rain," it means, "The last 100 times weather conditions were just like they are now, it rained 10 times."

WHAT DOES A CLOUD FEEL LIKE?

Silly question. You already know—or I should say, you already know if you've ever walked through a patch of fog. Fog is simply a cloud at ground level. Fog feels cool and damp; so do clouds.

HISTORY AND POLITICS

Do Indians really say "how" as a greeting?

Of course not. When Indians want to say "hello," they say "hello." On the other hand, this isn't one of those stories that the white man just made up. Certain tribes of Sioux Indians on the Great Plains did have a word that sounded something like "how," and often they did say it at the beginning of their conversations.

But the word didn't mean "hello." It meant something like "well" or "now then," as in, "Now then, paleface, what's this about selling Manhattan Island to you for $24?" The settlers, who didn't understand the Indian language, figured the word was meant as a greeting. Not too smart—I mean, for all the settlers knew, the Indians could have been saying, "In your face, dirtbag."

Is it true that "kangaroo" is really an aborigine word meaning "I don't know"?

No, although a lot of dopes think it is.

The story they tell goes like this. Captain James Cook

was an Englishman who explored much of the South Pacific in the 18th century. One day Cook was exploring Australia when he saw a funny-looking hopping critter with a pouch and a big tail.

When he asked one of the locals what the creature was, the man replied, "Kangaroo." According to legend, this was aborigine talk for "I don't know." Cook mistook this for the name of the animal, and his error has been with us ever since.

Pretty funny story, right? Too bad it's wrong. It *is* true that when some other explorers came back a few years later and asked the aborigines about the mysterious "kangaroo" Cook had described, the aborigines had no idea what the explorers were talking about.

But the reason the aborigines were puzzled is that the explorers were pronouncing "kangaroo" wrong. The explorers said kan-ga-ROO, but the proper way to say it was something like kang-OO-roo. Kang-OO-roo *is* an aborigine name for the animal we call a kangaroo.

Even if you didn't know all this, you'd still have to think the story was suspicious, because the same yarn turns up all over the world. For example, it's said that Nome, Alaska, got its name from an Eskimo phrase, "Ka-No-Me," meaning "I don't know." Yucatan, in southern Mexico, also supposedly means "I don't know."

Now, come on. The early explorers may not have been that bright (would *you* have gotten in a leaky tub to sail to America?), but they weren't complete idiots, either. Somebody's been putting us on.

IS IT TRUE THERE'S A CODE FOR STATUES OF GENERALS ON HORSES? I'VE HEARD THAT IF THE HORSE HAS ALL FOUR LEGS ON THE GROUND, THE RIDER DIED A NATURAL DEATH; IF THE HORSE HAS ONE LEG IN THE AIR, THE RIDER WAS WOUNDED IN BATTLE; AND IF THE HORSE HAS TWO LEGS IN THE AIR, THE RIDER WAS KILLED IN BATTLE.

As usual with these things, the horse-statue code is a myth. I dug out pictures of 18 horse statues in places from Chicago to St. Petersburg (the one in Russia), then tried to find out how the riders died. Result: zip. The riders died every which way, and for the most part it had nothing to do with how the horses in their statues were standing.

WHERE DID THE DOLLAR SIGN COME FROM?

Many people think the dollar sign ($) started out when someone wrote a U and an S on top of one another. Not so. The original dollar sign was an S with just *one* up-and-down stroke through it, not two.

Another theory is that the dollar sign was originally a P combined with an 8. That's because before the United States got around to minting its own money, it used Spanish money. The main Spanish coins were called "pieces of eight"—P8, get it? (You could saw them into eight pieces, or "bits," to make change. That's why we call a quarter "two bits" to this day.) But there's no evidence to back up the P8 theory.

The real explanation seems to be that the dollar sign was originally an abbreviation for "pesos."

The peso is the basic unit of Spanish money. In fact, the Spanish name for "piece of eight" is *peso de 8 reales*.

Two hundred years ago, when we were still using Spanish money (believe it or not, we didn't get around to minting our own money until 1794, nearly 20 years after the Declaration of Independence), it was only natural to shorten "200 pesos" to "ps 200." As time went on, the *P* and *S* began to get smushed together. Eventually people started writing the up-and-down stroke of the *P* on top of the *S*, and the dollar sign was born.

WHY DO OUTHOUSE DOORS HAVE CRESCENT MOONS ON THEM?

Let's get one thing straight: Most outhouses *don't* have crescent moons on them. I have a book with photos of outhouses—never mind *why* I have it—and most of the outhouses shown either have no symbol or a different symbol, such as a star. The idea that outhouses always sport moons appears to have been invented by cartoonists.

To be sure, some outhouses have moons. The symbol dates back to colonial times, when many people couldn't read. To help folks tell the men's outhouse from the women's, carpenters sometimes used symbols—a crescent moon for the women's outhouse and a radiant sun (that is, a sun with rays pointing out from it) for the men's. The sun is an ancient symbol for male, the moon an equally ancient symbol for female.

Why did people later come to believe the moon was the symbol for *all* outhouses? Nobody is sure, but one theory is that women saw to it that their outhouses were kept in good repair. Men, on the other hand, let theirs fall into wrack and ruin. Soon the only outhouses that were left were the ones with crescent moons. The cartoonists saw them and took it from there.

By the way, moons, suns, stars, and so on aren't just symbols. They also let fresh air get into the outhouse. If you've ever spent much time in an outhouse, you know that's a lot more important than the shape of the opening.

DID PEOPLE REALLY GET TARRED AND FEATHERED?

I'm afraid so. Exactly where and when the practice got started nobody knows, but it became popular around the time of the Revolutionary War, when patriots tarred and feathered those who favored the English side. The victim would be stripped naked, smeared with a coat of hot tar, and then covered with feathers, manure, or whatever else was handy. Sometimes a rope would be tied around the victim's neck so he could be paraded around before the townsfolk.

As you can imagine, getting tarred and feathered was painful and embarrassing. Some victims became badly blistered from the hot tar. On the other hand, it wasn't as bad as getting lynched (hanged). Mobs are said to have tarred and feathered people when they were feeling "playful" rather than vicious. But getting the stuff off still took hours of work with scrapers and turpentine.

Tarring and feathering continued off and on until early in this century. Eventually the practice died out, although one case was reported as late as 1950. One hopes it ended because people finally grew up, but maybe it was only because it got tougher to find tar and feathers. Not a classy part of our history, in any case.

WHO WOULD BECOME PRESIDENT IF BOTH THE PRESIDENT-ELECT AND THE VICE PRESIDENT-ELECT WERE TO DIE AFTER THE ELECTION IN NOVEMBER BUT BEFORE THE INAUGURATION IN JANUARY?

In case you were wondering, we say "president-elect" when somebody has been elected president but not yet sworn in. (If both the president and the vice president died *after* being sworn in, the rules are clear: the Speaker of the House would take over.)

Let's suppose it's the week after the election and both the president-elect and the vice president-elect are walking down the street. Suddenly a giant safe falls on them. Very sad, but from the nation's point of view, not a major crisis. That's because the electoral college hasn't met yet.

This may take some explanation. You may have the idea that Americans vote directly for their president. Strictly speaking, they don't. According to the U.S. Constitution, they vote for electors, and the electors choose the president a few weeks later.

The electors are pledged to certain candidates, and if they (the electors) get elected, they're expected to vote for those candidates when the time comes. But they don't *have* to.

If both the president-elect and the vice president-elect died before the electoral college met, one solution would be for the leaders of the winning party (the Democrats or the Republicans) to choose new candidates. The electors, who are supposed to be loyal to the party, would vote for these new candidates, and there you go.

But suppose the president-elect and vice president-elect both die *after* the electoral college vote, but before the inauguration. What happens then is anybody's guess—the situation is not covered by law. Congress would have to get together and cook something up fast. Considering how much goes wrong when Congress *isn't* under pressure, I shudder to think what would happen.

To avoid having to deal with such problems, the president and vice president never travel together, even after they're inaugurated. That way if an accident happens to the president, the vice president will still be around to carry on.

WHERE DID UNCLE SAM, THE CARTOON CHARACTER WHO SYMBOLIZES THE UNITED STATES, COME FROM?

Nobody is quite sure. I'll tell you the popular story, but don't let me catch you believing it.

Many claim the original Uncle Sam was Sam Wilson,

a meatpacker from Troy, New York. Wilson worked for Elbert Anderson, who had a contract to supply rations to the U.S. Army during the War of 1812.

All the meat sent to the army had "E.A.—U.S." stamped on it, which stood for "Elbert Anderson— United States," of course. But when Sam Wilson's employees asked him what "E.A.—U.S." stood for, he told them it was "Elbert Anderson and Uncle Sam," Uncle Sam being Wilson himself. The workers thought this was pretty funny and spread the joke far and wide.

It's a good story. You'll even find it repeated in the *Encyclopedia Britannica*, which says Congress passed a resolution in 1961 recognizing Wilson as the original Uncle Sam. But it has a lot of holes in it.

For one thing, it's hard to believe anybody could be so out of it they'd have to ask what "U.S." stood for. What's more, even though Sam Wilson was well known in Troy, nobody in town seems to have heard the story until many years after the War of 1812.

When Sam Wilson died in 1854, none of the Troy newspaper writers mentioned anything about his having been the original Uncle Sam. But the papers did reprint two death notices about Wilson that had first appeared in Albany. These *did* mention the Uncle Sam story. It seems suspicious that out-of-town newspapers would know the story while the local papers did not. Some think the explanation is that the out-of-towners made it up.

So what's the truth? The best guess is that Uncle Sam was dreamed up by some unknown wiseguy. The nickname became popular around 1812 when it was used sarcastically by "peace" newspapers—that is, those that opposed the United States' involvement in the War of

1812. It was only after the war that the name began to be used by everyone.

The idea of Uncle Sam as a tall, thin man with a white beard and top hat came later still. Cartoonists from the British magazine *Punch* began drawing Uncle Sam that way from the 1830s onward. But it wasn't until the famous cartoonist Thomas Nast got into the act in the 1870s that the modern cartoon image of Uncle Sam became firmly fixed in everyone's mind.[1] Today it's hard to imagine Uncle Sam looking any other way.

WHY DO THE ENGLISH DRIVE ON THE LEFT SIDE OF THE ROAD, WHILE AMERICANS DRIVE ON THE RIGHT?

Once upon a time, everybody drove the English way— that is, on the left side of the road. There was good reason for this. Centuries ago you never knew if the person coming toward you was friend or foe. Since most people were right-handed, they would edge toward the left side of the road so that they could grab their weapons with their right hands if they had to. (See illustration.)

Traveling on the left became official (sort of) in 1300 A.D. when the Pope declared that pilgrims heading to Rome should keep left to avoid traffic jams. People continued to keep left for hundreds of years afterward.

But in the late 1700s, this began to change in the United States due to the popularity of **Conestoga** (kon-

---

[1]Nast, incidentally, also invented the Republican elephant, made the Democratic donkey popular, and created the present-day image of Santa Claus as a jolly fat man in a red suit.

eh-STO-guh) wagons. These large horse-drawn wagons, first used in Pennsylvania's Conestoga Valley, had no seat for a driver. Instead the driver rode the last horse on the left-hand side so he could whip the horses using his right arm. (See illustration.)

If you're sitting on the left-hand horse, it's important for you to pass on the right. That way you can look down from where you're sitting and make sure your wheels aren't going to hit the wheels of wagons heading in the opposite direction from you.

Left side of road   **Right arm**

Strangers meeting on the road in the Middle Ages kept to the left so that they could be ready to defend themselves.

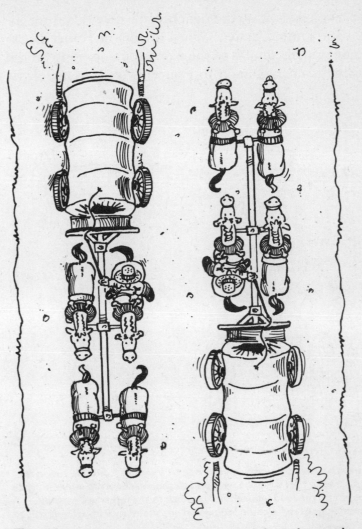

The driver of a Conestoga wagon rode on the left rear horse so he could whip horses with his right arm. He kept to the right so that when he passed other wagons he could look down, and make sure that his wagon's wheels wouldn't hit those of the wagon coming from the opposite direction.

Soon passing on the right became common throughout the United States.[2] When drivers in France began using wagons similar to the Conestogas, passing on the right became common in France as well. Many of the

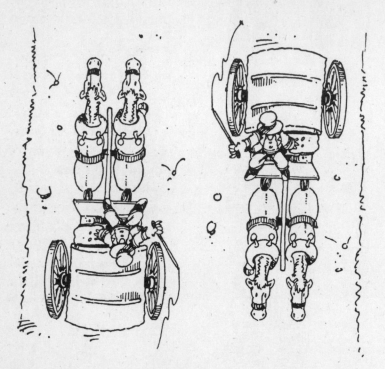

The driver of an English wagon rode on a seat in front. He sat on the right side so that when he whipped the horses the whip wouldn't get caught on the load behind him. He kept to the left when passing other wagons so he could look down and make sure his wheels stayed clear.

[2]Of course, *passing* on the right isn't quite the same thing as *driving* on the right—that is, staying on the right side of the road whether you're passing or not. That didn't really happen until highway officials began painting lane stripes in the 20th century. But you see how things got started.

countries conquered by France during the Napoleonic wars also switched to driving on the right.

The English, however, used a smaller wagon, one that was smaller and had a seat up front for the driver. The drivers sat on the right side so that when they whipped the horses, their whips wouldn't get tangled behind them in the wagon. (See illustration.)

Naturally, since they were on the right side of the wagon, English drivers preferred to keep on the left side of the road, so they too could look down to make sure their wheels kept clear of passing wagons. And since they'd been driving on the left side for hundreds of years, why change? They're still doing it that way, as are many of their former colonies, such as Australia and India.

Today, driving on the right (the way Americans do it) has become the most common method throughout the world. Of the five countries with the most people, three drive on the right (the United States, Russia, and China), and two drive on the left (Indonesia and India). Someday maybe we'll get organized and everybody will drive on the same side. Until then, do like Mom said: Look *both* ways before you cross the street.

HOW COME THERE ARE 5,280 FEET TO A MILE? WHY NOT SOME MORE CONVENIENT NUMBER, LIKE 5,000?

Blame our friends the English. They originally got the idea of the mile from the Romans, who once ruled part of

Britain. The Romans had a measure called the **mille passuum** (ME-lay PA-soo-em), literally, "a thousand paces." Each pace consisted of five Roman feet, for a total of 5,000 feet per mile. Very easy to remember.

Unfortunately, the English couldn't leave well enough alone. Besides the mile, they had a measurement called the **furlong,** which was used to measure farmers' fields. A furlong is said to have been the distance a horse could pull a plow in a straight line before having to rest. It was 660 feet long.

The English wanted to have eight furlongs to the mile. Trouble was, 8 times 660 was 5,280. So somebody said, "Look, we can't have two different measurements for the mile. We have to pick one or the other. What is the obvious, sensible thing to do?"

Simple—make the mile 5,000 feet long and shave the furlong down so you could still fit eight into a mile. The English knew this. However, being English, they did exactly the opposite. They made the mile 5,280 feet long.

To be fair about it, they did have a reason for this. Most property deeds at the time had been figured out in furlongs that were 660 feet long. If furlongs were suddenly shortened, a lot of farmers would have been pretty mad. But hey, it's always something.

WHAT IS THE ORIGIN OF THE WORD "OKAY" (OK)?

Dozens of theories about the origin of "okay" have been suggested. Here are a few of them:

• It comes from the Choctaw Indian word "okeh," meaning "yes."

• It stands for Obediah Kelly, a railroad freight agent who used to mark his initials on important papers to show that everything was in order.

• It comes from the name of the Haitian port Aux Cayes, which is pronounced "okay." The town of Aux Cayes was said to be famous among sailors for its rum. When sailors liked something, they got into the habit of saying, "You know, this is really *Aux Cayes* stuff"—that is, it was good quality.

I could go on, but you get the idea.

The *real* explanation was discovered by a Columbia University professor named Allen Walker Read. He proved that "OK" originally stood for "oll korrect," a comical way of writing "all correct."

In the late 1830s, it seems, there was a fad among newspaper writers to invent comical initials to use in their stories. This may not seem like an especially hilarious idea today, but people had simple tastes back then.

Many of these initials involved misspellings. You had OK, "oll korrect"; KY, "know yuse" (no use); KG, "know go" (no go); NS, "nuff said" (enough said); and so on.

Most of the comical initials didn't last. OK was different, partly because it came in handy in conversation. But there was another reason as well.

In 1840 Martin Van Buren was running for president. He was called "Old Kinderhook," after the town in New York where he was born. The initials of "Old Kinderhook," are, of course, "OK."

Van Buren's supporters called their political club the

"OK Club," and "OK" became their war cry. They would shout it at rallies or whenever they were out beating up their opponents, which was a common method of campaigning in those days.

Van Buren's enemies, meanwhile, began trying to use OK against him. They said it stood for "Orfully Konfused," or "Often Kontradicts," or "Out of Kash, Out of Kredit, and Out of Klothes." By the time the campaign was over, everybody had heard of OK, and many were using it to mean "all right," just as we do today. But they had already forgotten where the term came from and what it stood for.

Now you know. Don't let anyone tell you different—okay?

How DID THE TELEPHONE COMPANY ASSIGN THE AREA CODES?

If you've ever looked at an area code map, you've probably wondered: How on earth did they assign the area codes, anyway—throw darts? The numbers are completely scrambled.

Take Milwaukee, for example. It's 414. You'd figure 414 would come in between 413 and 415. It does, sort of. The only problem is, the 413 area is western Massachusetts, 1,000 miles east, and 415 is San Francisco, 2,000 miles west. 205 is Alabama, 206 is Seattle, and 207 is Maine—about as far apart as you can get.

But have no fear. The situation isn't as confused as it

***On** a rotary dial phone, it takes longer to dial "9" than "1" because the dial has to rotate back to its starting point.*

looks. Area codes were assigned in 1948, before the invention of Touch-Tone telephones. All phones then had rotary dials, as in the illustration above.[3]

Dialing an 8 or a 9 on a rotary phone is slow. You have to rotate the dial until you get to the finger stop, then wait till the dial spins back to its starting point. Dialing 919 takes a lot longer than 212.

Phone company experts called numbers like 212 "low dial-pull" numbers, because you didn't have to pull the dial very far when you used them. When they assigned the area codes, they gave the low dial-pull numbers to large cities. New York got 212, Los Angeles got 213, and Chicago got 312.

Millions of people called those cities every day. The

[3]You may recognize these phones from *The Flintstones*, which is about the last time they were used.

faster each caller was able to dial his number, the less time the phone company's switching machines would be tied up making the connection. The faster each switching machine worked, the fewer machines the phone company had to buy. In short, the area codes were assigned the way they were so the phone company could save money.

A few years later, Touch-Tone phones were invented. On a Touch-Tone phone, all the area codes could be dialed (pressed, actually) equally fast. Suddenly, all that stuff about dial-pulls was out the window.

Today the only concern when assigning new area codes is to make them as different as possible from neighboring codes, so people won't confuse the numbers. That's why when New York City (212) was divided into two area codes, the new code was 718. The new code added to Los Angeles (213) was 818, and the new code for Chicago (312) was 708.

Of course, nothing's perfect. The area-code system is designed to make it hard to get the numbers mixed up. But if you do anyway, you're in big trouble. If you try to dial Miami (305) and punch 304 instead, your call will wind up in West Virginia. So be careful the next time you dial to order pizza.

How come there's no Q and Z on the telephone dial?

When I was in high school we thought it was really hilarious to tell some guy he'd win $1,000 if he called QUincy

5-2000 within five minutes. (This was back when phone numbers all started with folksy names instead of numbers.) Naturally the guy would rush to the phone, only to find he couldn't dial the number because there was no Q on the dial. Big laughs!

Okay, so we were easily amused. The question remains, *why* isn't there any Q or Z on the phone dial?

Here's the simple answer: Because zero and 1 couldn't have letters assigned to them. Since there were only ten numbers on the dial to start with, that left eight that could have letters assigned. Eight times three is 24. There are 26 letters in the alphabet, so two had to get cut. Q and Z were the unlucky pair.

Fine. But why couldn't letters be assigned to 0 and 1?

Zero and 1 are "flag" numbers, often used for special purposes. Zero is used to reach the operator. One is used for special numbers like 911, emergency service, and 411, directory assistance.

Another important use of flag numbers is in making long-distance calls. Until recently, all the area codes had either a 1 or a 0 in the middle position—212, 609, and so on. That told the phone company's switching machines, "This is going to be a long-distance call, not a local call."

Suppose the letter A had been assigned to 1, and you were dialing AArdvark 1-2345. You started off dialing 111. The switching machine would think this was a long-distance call, when all you wanted was to call over to the other side of town. Chaos! So, no letters were assigned to 0 and 1.

But now there's another problem.

There are only a handful of area code numbers left. Or

at least there were. Luckily, the phone company has changed over to a new system for long distance. You dial 1 first, then the area code, then the number.

The 1 at the beginning tells the switching machine, "This is a long-distance call." That means the middle number of the area code no longer needs to be limited to 0 or 1. Now we can have 449, 732, whatever—a total of 692 new area codes in all. That ought to hold us for a while.

WHY ARE KENTUCKY, MASSACHUSETTS, PENNSYLVANIA, AND VIRGINIA CALLED COMMONWEALTHS RATHER THAN STATES?

People in Chicago live in the state of Illinois. People in Boston, on the other hand, live in the commonwealth of Massachusetts. Commonwealth may sound a little classier, but legally there's no difference between a commonwealth and a state.

So why use different names? Mostly because "commonwealth" was an important word in history. Back in the 1600s, a commonwealth was a venture in which everybody got together and worked for the common good, or "weal." That was a good description of the first colonies, where people had to work together or die in the untamed new land.

The first settlers at Jamestown, Virginia, called their little settlement a commonwealth from the day they arrived in 1607. It was only natural that they'd want to continue calling it a commonwealth when Virginia became a part of the United States after the Revolutionary War.

Folks in Massachusetts liked the idea of working for the common good, too. Another reason they favored "commonwealth" was that they were opposed to being ruled by kings, and commonwealth sounded more democratic.

Today "commonwealth" means something different. It's a territory that isn't a state but isn't an independent country either. The island of Puerto Rico is a commonwealth. Maybe someday it'll be a state. But you folks in the commonwealths of Kentucky, Massachusetts, Pennsylvania, and Virginia needn't worry—you're already in.

WHY DO WE CALL THE DOLLAR A "DOLLAR" AND A BUCK A "BUCK"?

"Dollar" comes from "Joachimsthaler," a coin made in the 16th century at a mint near a silver mine in Joachimsthal, in what is now Czechoslovakia. "Joachimsthal" means "Joachim's dale," dale being another word for valley.

"Joachimsthaler" was soon shortened to "thaler." The Dutch made it into "daler," and the English finished the job by making it into "dollar."

The name "thaler" or "dollar" has been used for different coins at different times. In colonial America it was given to the Spanish dollar, a large silver coin known as a "piece of eight" that was widely used for trade even after the Revolutionary War. When the American government established its own money in 1785, it was only natural that the basic unit of money should be called the "dollar." (No dollars were actually minted until 1794— till then we just kept using the Spanish stuff.)

The origin of "buck," the slang term for dollar, is a little less clear. The best theory is that "buck" comes from the frontier practice of trading goods to the Indians for buckskins—that is, the skin of a male deer. If an Indian with some skins to unload came to a trading post and asked what a certain item cost, the trader might say, "It'll cost you two bucks," meaning two buckskins. Later the term came to signify dollars. Just as well. Dollar bills may not be as much fun as buckskin, but they're a lot easier to fit in your wallet.

IS IT TRUE THE ANCIENT EGYPTIANS USED A SECRET METHOD TO PRESERVE MUMMIES THAT MODERN SCIENCE HAS NEVER BEEN ABLE TO DISCOVER?

This is one of those things teachers tell you to liven up a tour of a natural history museum. But it's not true. The ancient Egyptians didn't use any secret methods to preserve mummies—at least nothing that worked.

What really kept mummies from decaying into dust was the hot, dry climate of Egypt. If the Egyptians had had to work in the damp climate of northern Europe or

America, few if any mummies would have survived. There'd be no King Tut and no classic movies like *Curse of the Mummy's Tomb*. Good thing the Egyptians liked it where they were.

WHY ARE STOPLIGHTS RED, YELLOW, AND GREEN? WHY NOT SOME OTHER COLORS?

For a darn good reason, as we shall see.

Early traffic officials borrowed the red-yellow-green code from the railroads, which used it for the track signals needed to control trains.

The railroads chose red for the "stop" signal because for thousands of years it had been the signal for danger. Red is the color of blood. So if you want to tell people to stop lest they face death and destruction, red makes sense.

But the other colors were pretty much pulled out of a hat. In fact, when the railroads first got started in the 1830s and 1840s, the color for "caution" was green and the color for "go" was "clear"—white, in other words.

After a while, it became apparent that these colors presented some serious problems. For one thing, it was easy to mistake an ordinary white light (say, a street lamp) for a "go" signal.

But even worse things could happen. The story is told that once the red glass lens fell out of a stop signal, showing the ordinary white light bulb behind. A train engineer, seeing the white light, thought he was looking at a "go" signal rather than a "stop" and failed to slow his train. The result was a terrible crash.

So the railroads decided to change to a more foolproof system—red for "stop," green for "go," and yellow for "caution." If an engineer saw a white light where a signal was supposed to be, he would know something was wrong, and he'd stop to check things out.

Traffic engineers, knowing a good thing when they saw one, borrowed the red-yellow-green system for use in stoplights. The first electric traffic signals, which were installed in Cleveland in 1914, used just two lights, red and green. But yellow was added within a few years and it's been that way ever since.

Yellow still means "caution," by the way. I feel it's important to mention this. Many drivers these days seem to think it means "go for it."

HOW IT WORKS

10

HOW COME IT HURTS WHEN YOU CHEW ON ALUMINUM SPITBALLS?

What, you never noticed this? Then either (1) you never chewed an aluminum spitball (definitely an experience you don't want to repeat), or (2) you don't have any silver tooth fillings.[1]

The awful truth is, aluminum and silver together create a *tiny electric battery*. The electricity flows from the aluminum to the silver by way of your spit. It's not enough juice to jump your folks' car in the winter, but it's definitely enough to hurt.

SUPPOSE YOU HAD A GUN. YOU AIM IT PERFECTLY LEVEL AND FIRE. AT THE SAME INSTANT, YOU DROP A BULLET FROM THE SAME HEIGHT AS THE GUN. WHICH BULLET HITS THE GROUND FIRST?[2]

You'd probably guess that the dropped bullet hits the ground first, because it travels a shorter distance. Wrong.

---

[1] You say you want to experience aluminum spitballs firsthand? Wad up a tiny piece of aluminum foil (a piece of a foil gum wrapper will do, but regular aluminum foil works better). Pop it in your mouth and chomp away. See? Next time take my word for it.

[2] This is *not* an experiment to try at home—or anywhere!

The bullets hit the ground *at the same time*.

What makes the shot bullet go forward is a **horizontal** (hor-uh-ZAHN-tull—that is, sideways) force, namely, the exploding gunpowder. The only downward force acting on the bullets is gravity. It acts equally on both the dropped bullet and the shot bullet. Equal forces cause equal results, so the bullets hit the ground together. (See illustration.)

There is one complication.[3] If the shot bullet goes far

A *bullet fired from a gun and a bullet dropped from the same height will hit the ground at the same time—unless the shot bullet travels so far that the earth begins to curve away from it. In that case the dropped bullet hits the ground first.*

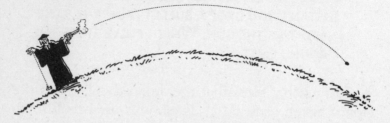

[3]Two complications, actually. Some folks say the drag of the air on the shot bullet would make it hit the ground at a different time than the dropped bullet. We'll get this cleared up eventually.

enough, the earth begins to curve away from it. (See illustration.) In that case, the dropped bullet hits the ground first.

This point is worth remembering because, while most high school science teachers know the simple answer to the dropped bullet question, they forget about the complication. When this comes up in high school physics (and believe me, it will), you'll have a chance to sound like Einstein.

How come you can see through glass?

To understand this, you need to know another Weird Fact: *Glass is not a solid*. It's just a very thick liquid, like extra-hard Jell-O. Don't believe me? Go find a window. Now wait one billion years. See what I mean? The glass has flowed out of the window frame and gotten all over the carpet.

Actually, a lot of times you don't even have to wait one billion years. You may notice that very old windows often are thicker on the bottom than the top. That's because the glass has oozed downhill over the years.

Basically, you can see through glass for the same reason you can see through any liquid, such as water. The molecules are so loosely spaced they don't block the light. What's more, there's very little in glass to *reflect* light, as in metals; to *bend* it, as in crystals;[4] or to *absorb* it. So the light just zips right through.

---

[4]To clarify, light does bend slightly when it passes from air to glass, and from glass back to air. That's what makes eyeglasses possible.

Is it possible to make a machine that would produce more energy than it would use up?

Despite what you may have seen on TV, no. On the other hand, there is one machine that, once started, will run for years without additional energy.

What we're talking about here is what's known as a **perpetual** (per-PET-chew-ull) **motion machine.** As the name suggests ("perpetual" means endless), perpetual motion machines can run forever without fuel. People have been trying to invent them for thousands of years, for the obvious reason that, hey, you'd sure save on the gas bill.

The trouble is that perpetual motion machines violate two basic laws of the universe, namely, (1) you don't get something for nothing, and (2) anything that starts will eventually stop.

But what about those guys on TV? They claim their machines produce more energy than they use.

Well, look, getting on TV is not that difficult. Even I've been on TV. All getting on TV proves is that you're witty, charming, good-loo...—sorry, got distracted. Anyway, when scientists test those contraptions that are shown on TV, they always end up finding out the machines use more energy than they produce.

The basic problem is **friction.** If you've ever scraped your foot on the ground to slow down a wagon or a bike, you've seen friction in action. Friction will cause everything to stop sooner or later.

Still, it might be a *lot* later. Remember I said there was one machine that would run almost forever without using energy? That machine is a satellite circling the earth.

Friction from particles floating in space will eventually slow all satellites to the point that they fall into the earth's atmosphere and burn up. But if we let them, some satellites will circle the earth for thousands of years. That's about as close to a perpetual motion machine as you can get.

CAN SOAP EVER GET DIRTY? SUPPOSE YOU WASHED SOME DIRT; WHAT WOULD BE LEFT? HOW WOULD YOU KNOW WHEN IT WAS CLEAN?

I get a lot of questions like this. People are so immature. The truth is, soap *has* to get dirty; otherwise, it wouldn't work.

What's more, soap doesn't work on just any old dirt; it works on *greasy* dirt. Wash a chunk of garden dirt with soap and you'll get the same thing as if you washed it with water—mud.

The real reason you need soap is something we talked about in an earlier chapter: *Oil and water don't mix*. If you pour oil into a dish of water, the oil just wads up into little balls and floats.

So, while nongreasy dirt will come off with nothing more than water and a good scrubbing, greasy dirt is a different story. Water alone has no effect on grease. That's why you need soap.

Soap works because its molecules are two-faced. One side is attractive to grease—in fact, the grease would rather stick to soap than whatever it was on in the first place. Meanwhile, the other side of the soap molecule is attractive to water.

Say you're washing a dirty shirt. When the soap floats by, the dirt drops the shirt like a hot potato and hooks up with the soap. Meanwhile, the other end of the soap molecule is attracted to the water. The dirt winds up surrounded by soap molecules, which in turn are surrounded by water. Drain off the water and it's ta-ta dirt.

How do planes fly?

If you've ever flown in a plane, you know the feeling. You look out the window and you see these little wings, a lot of sky, and not a whole lot else. The thought goes through your mind: Okay, what's *really* holding this thing up?

Answer: thin air. Not much comfort, but it's the best I can do.

The reason air can hold you up has to do with the **Bernoulli** (ber-NEW-lee) **principle.** The Bernoulli principle is a little complicated, but for our purposes what it says is this: If the *speed* of flowing air *increases*, the *pressure* of the air *decreases*. (See illustration.)

Airplanes use the Bernoulli principle to fly. To do this, airplane wings are made in a special shape called an **airfoil.** From the side the wing appears as shown in the other illustration on the next page.

Notice how the wing is flat on the bottom, but rounded on the top. When the plane's engines pull it through the sky, air flows above and below the wing. Because the top of the wing is rounded, the air above must travel farther than the air below before it reaches the back edge.

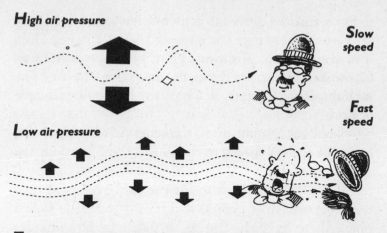

High air pressure

Slow speed

Fast speed

Low air pressure

The higher the speed of the air, the lower its pressure.

That means it has to move faster.

Higher speed means lower pressure. So the air above presses down less than the air below presses up. The difference in pressure forces the wing up. We say that the wing has generated **lift.**

Sounds fishy, you say? Well, it does seem a little thin to build an entire industry around. But here are some tricks

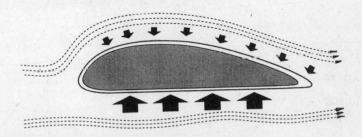

Airfoil. The air traveling over the wing has farther to go, so it must move faster in order to keep up with the air traveling under the wing. It presses down much less than the air beneath the wing is pressing up, so the wing rises.

to prove that the Bernoulli principle really does work.

Get a piece of paper no larger than 6 by 9 inches. Hold it to your mouth, as shown. Now, blow across the top. Contrary to what you'd expect, the paper will *rise*. The moving air has created lift. That's the Bernoulli principle at work.

Next, get a small card (a business card is best) and bend the ends as shown in the illustration. Then lay the card on the table.

Now, dare somebody to flip the card over using only their breath. Most people will blow their little hearts out, only to have the card stick to the tabletop harder

The Bernoulli principle in action: blowing across the top of a sheet of paper makes the paper rise.

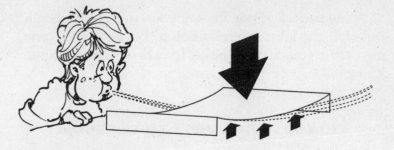

It's impossible to flip the card over by blowing underneath it. Because of the Bernoulli principle, the card clings tightly to the table.

than ever.

Why doesn't the card flip over? Because of the Bernoulli principle. The fast-moving stream of air passing under the card has lower pressure than the still air above. So the card is actually forced down, not up.

How can you get the card to flip over? Easy. Blow straight down at the table a few inches away from the card, as shown. The air will curl under the card and push up, flipping it over.

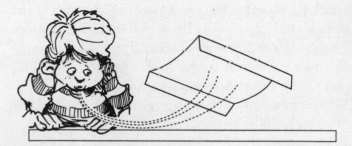

To flip the card over, blow straight down a few inches away.

Card tricks may not convince you that the Bernoulli principle can keep an airplane aloft. But at least this one might distract you until you get back down to the ground.

How do stunt planes fly upside down?

If you were paying attention during that last answer (and I will be very hurt if you weren't), you know the Bernoulli principle works because the flat part of the airplane wing is on the bottom and the round side is on top.

But then you go to the air show and you see stunt planes flying upside down. "How can this be?" you ask. "When a plane is upside down, the flat part of the wing is on top and the round part is on the bottom. Why doesn't the plane fall out of the sky?"

Well, actually, I was holding out on you a bit. The Bernoulli effect isn't the only thing keeping the plane in the air. There's also something called **angle of attack.**

We may show this by means of the following experiment. Next time you're in the car going down the highway, stick your hand out the window.[5] Feel the rush of air? Now angle your hand upward as shown in the illustration.

See how the wind forces your hand upward? The steep "angle of attack"—that is, the angle at which your hand cuts into the wind—has given your hand lift.

When planes take off, they angle their wings steeply, too. The extra lift helps them get off the ground.

A steep angle of attack also enables a stunt plane to fly upside down. After the pilot flips the plane over, he posi-

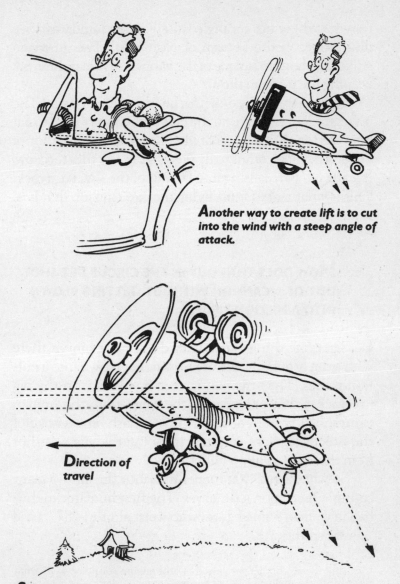

Another way to create lift is to cut into the wind with a steep angle of attack.

Direction of travel

Stunt planes can fly upside down by heading into the wind at a steep angle.

tions it so the wings are angled just like your hand was. (See illustration on the bottom of page 195.) The airstream strikes the bottom surface of the wings and forces them up, keeping the plane in the air.

You can fly upside down for quite a while this way. The only problem (apart from the fact that it's very hard to eat popcorn) is that a steep angle of attack creates a lot of **drag.**[6] The plane tends to fly pretty slow. If it flies too slow, it **stalls** (stops), causing it to fall out of the sky like a rock. This is what makes stunt flying the exciting job that it is.

How DOES THAT GUY IN THE CIRCUS GET SHOT OUT OF A CANNON WITHOUT GETTING BLOWN INTO A MILLION PIECES?

Let's get one thing clear. They don't pack him in there with a ton of gunpowder, or he *would* get blown into a million pieces. The only gunpowder involved is in the big firecracker that explodes at the same time the human cannonball is launched. The noise, flash, and smoke of the firecracker fool you into thinking the guy was shot from the cannon like a bullet.

So what actually launches him into the air—a giant spring? Once upon a time, yes. The first human cannonball, a woman named Zazel who went aloft in 1877, used "elastic springs."

---

[6] Actually, there's another problem, too—the engine's oil pump won't work right and the pistons will lock up. You have to make sure you've got a plane with a special engine to avoid this problem.

Today, the preferred method is compressed air. Inside the barrel of the cannon is a person-sized hollow cylinder with no top. The human cannonball climbs into this cylinder just before launch. While the cannon is raised to the proper angle, the cylinder slides down the barrel to the bottom.

At the proper moment, a huge amount of compressed air is released behind the cylinder. (Ever use a pea shooter? Same idea.) The cylinder rockets to the top of the barrel, where it stops. The person inside doesn't. He or she flies as much as a hundred feet to a waiting net.

At least the human cannonball *hopes* the net is waiting. A lot of times it isn't, or rather, it's not waiting in the spot that the human cannonball happens to land. Of some 50 people who have been shot from cannons over the years, about 30 have been killed, mostly because they missed the net.

Even if they avoid the big splat, the shock of launch makes many human cannonballs black out in flight. Getting shot out of a gun may look like fun, but there are easier ways to make a living.

Is it really possible to walk on a bed of red-hot coals and not get burned?

You bet. Not that I have; one thing I'm not is stupid. But lots of other people have. While some have gotten blistered and a few have been badly burned, most get through fine.

How can this be? Some firewalk "experts" would

have you believe it's because of the power of mind over matter. What's more, they'll charge you pots of money to teach you the secret.

Firewalk promoters sponsor big meetings where they tell a roomful of people to believe in the strength of their inner being and stuff like that. The climax of the evening is walking in your bare feet over a bed of hot coals 3 feet wide and 10 feet long.

I don't have much use for stunts like this. It's not that firewalking is a fake. You *can* walk across those coals without getting burned. But no preparation is necessary. (Not that I'm suggesting *you* try it, you understand.)

Two things make firewalking possible. The first is something called the **Leidenfrost** (LIE-den-frost) **effect,** also known as the "sizzle effect." When you're standing there waiting to hike across the coals, chances are your body is sweating buckets, your feet most of all. When you walk on the hot coals, the thin layer of moisture on the soles of your feet instantly turns to vapor. The vapor protects you long enough for you to get to the other side.

The second thing is that wood is a poor conductor of heat. Heat travels through wood so slowly that if you move fast, not enough will reach your feet to burn them.

Firewalk promoters use a few additional tricks to make firewalking even safer. The first is that they don't add more coals as the night wears on, so the last person to scamper across is basically walking on cold ashes. Second, they may direct you to walk over a bed of grass before heading out over the coals. The grass coats the soles of your feet with extra moisture.

None of this changes the basic fact: You *can* walk

across hot coals in your bare feet. But it's also easy to get badly burned, so don't try it on your own.

WHY DOES THE ACTION IN THOSE OLD SILENT MOVIES SEEM SO FAST AND JERKY?

Two reasons, actually. One is that many silent movies were made at much slower speeds than "talkies." On average, silent movies were meant to run through the projector at about 16 frames per second. (Some were a lot faster, some even slower.) When they're run through today's projectors, which operate at 24 frames per second, the action is speeded up by 50 percent.

The other reason the action is so fast, at least in old comedies, is that it's funnier that way. The Keystone Kops films—the ones with lots of chases involving carloads of old-time cops waving billy clubs—were shot at very slow speeds on purpose. Even when projected at 16 frames per second, the action was frantic. When we see those movies today, we think the jerky movement is funny. But people thought the same thing in 1915.

WHEN THE BAD GUYS ARE CHASING THE STAGECOACH IN ONE OF THOSE OLD MOVIES, HOW COME THE WHEELS OF THE STAGECOACH APPEAR TO SLOW DOWN AND START SPINNING BACKWARD?

What we have here is what's called a **stroboscopic** (STROW-buh-skop-ick) **illusion**—strobe effect, for short. It's caused by the shutter of the movie camera.

A movie doesn't really show continuous action. Actually, it consists of a series of ordinary still photos strung together. When the photos are quickly flashed on the screen one after another, your eye runs them all together to create the illusion of continuous action. (See illustration.)

A movie camera takes 24 pictures per second. Suppose you're filming a wheel that turns 24 times per second. When the camera shutter opens the first time, let's say the wheel is in position 1, with the letter A on top. (See illustration at top of next page.)

Then the shutter closes. In 1/24th of a second, the time before the shutter opens again, the wheel makes one full turn, as shown. By the time the shutter opens again, the wheel is in the same position it was in during the first shot. So when the movie is played back, the wheel appears to be standing still.

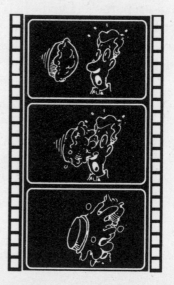

Movies create the illusion of motion by stringing together a series of still photos.

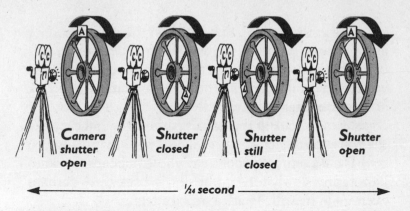

Camera shutter open **Shutter closed** **Shutter still closed** **Shutter open**

←——————— ¹⁄₂₄ second ———————→

*S*trobe effect. When the film is viewed, the letter A on the rotating wheel appears not to move.

Now, suppose the wheel is turning slightly slower than 24 times per second. In that case, it isn't going fast enough to make a full turn before the shutter opens again. (See illustration below.)

When the movie is played back, the wheel appears to be rotating slightly backward. That's what happens to the wheel of the stagecoach.

Sometimes you can see a strobe illusion without hav-

Open Closed Closed Open Closed Closed Open Closed Closed Open

|←—— ¹⁄₂₄ second ——→|←—— ¹⁄₂₄ second ——→|←—— ¹⁄₂₄ second ——→|

*R*everse rotation effect. As wheel turns slightly slower than 24 times per second, it appears to rotate backwards when film is viewed.

ing to be at the movies. Street lights (the mercury vapor and sodium vapor kind, anyway) flash 120 times per second. That's much too fast for you to notice directly. But if you're in a car going down the highway some night, look at the hubcaps of the other cars as they pass by. (Specifically, look at the darker parts of the hubcap, like the bolts; the reflections off the shiny parts may throw you off.) You'll eventually spot a car whose hubcaps appear to be rotating slowly forward or slowly backward, perhaps even standing still. That's a strobe effect.

WHY ARE THERE LINES IN THE SIDEWALK?

Simple. (Isn't everything?) When concrete dries, it shrinks, and when it shrinks, it cracks. If the concrete didn't have lines in it, the cracks would form just any old place and the concrete would look terrible. As it is, the cracks follow the lines, because that's where the slab is thinnest, and they look neater. In other words, the lines in a sidewalk are a way of making the best of a bad situation. Much of life is like this.

WHY DO OFFICE BUILDINGS AND DEPARTMENT STORES HAVE REVOLVING DOORS? WHAT'S WRONG WITH THE REGULAR KIND?

Come on, don't you want a little variety in your life? Besides, revolving doors serve an important purpose—

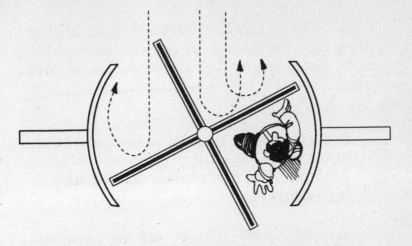

A revolving door prevents air from rushing in or out of a building.

they're energy-saving devices.

The air pressure inside a big building is often different from the air pressure outside. For example, in a tall building, warm air rises up the elevator shafts.[7] Cool air is pulled in at ground level to replace the warm air. If you opened an ordinary door leading outside, you'd get a blast of wind blowing in.

In other buildings, the wind blows in the opposite direction. Why? Who knows. The point is, the wind blowing in or out of the building might be enough to knock somebody over.

Worse, it wastes energy. Say it's the middle of January. You open an ordinary door that leads outside. Cold air rushes in (or heated air rushes out), the furnace kicks in, and another 20 bucks' worth of energy goes up the chimney.

[7]We talk about why warm air rises on pages 145-146.

Revolving doors prevent this by making certain there is never a clear path from the inside of the building to the outside. (See illustration.) Air can't rush in or out, so no energy is lost.

How come some electrical plugs have one blade wider than the other one? Sometimes you can't even stick the plug into a socket.

The electrical industry is trying to *help* you, you ingrate. What you're talking about is what's called a **polarizing** (POE-luh-ri-zing) **plug.** You find them on lamps, televisions, blow dryers, and many other devices.

Polarizing plugs are supposed to be safer because they can fit into the socket only one way. (Sometimes they won't fit into the socket *any* way. Can't get much safer than that, can you?)

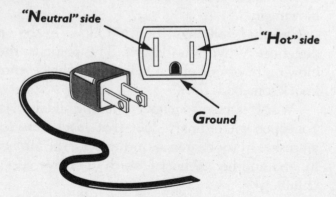

"**N**eutral" side · "**H**ot" side · Ground

Polarizing plugs have one blade wider than the other, to make it less likely that you'll get a dangerous electric shock.

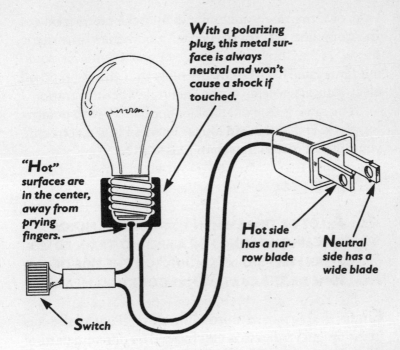

With a polarizing plug, this metal surface is always neutral and won't cause a shock if touched.

"**H**ot" surfaces are in the center, away from prying fingers.

Hot side has a narrow blade

Neutral side has a wide blade

Switch

Most electrical sockets these days have two slots plus a half-round hole in the middle. (See illustration.) The half-round hole is the "ground," which we don't have to worry about. The narrower of the two slots is the "hot" side, and the wider one is the "neutral" side.

If you were to shove a piece of metal into the neutral slot, nothing would happen. But if you were to shove it into the hot slot, you'd get a jolt of volts that would knock you across the room—and possibly kill you.

Why is this distinction important? Because when a light bulb is screwed into a socket, part of the metal base remains visible. Suppose the base were connected to the hot side of the wall plug. If you accidentally touched the base, or if the base somehow touched the metal frame of the lamp and you touched that, you could be in for a shock.

If the lamp has a polarizing plug, though, any exposed electrical parts will always be "neutral." (See illustration.)

The same is true of all other appliances with polarizing plugs. That doesn't mean it's impossible to electrocute yourself, but it's tougher than it used to be.

A LOT OF TIMES WHEN YOU'RE AT A RAILROAD CROSSING WAITING FOR A FREIGHT TRAIN TO GO BY YOU SEE "DO NOT HUMP" ON THE SIDE OF SOME OF THE CARS. WHAT DOES THAT MEAN?

One of the big jobs in railroading is to sort out all the cars in the freight yard so that cars headed for different parts of the country get put with the right trains. You can do this

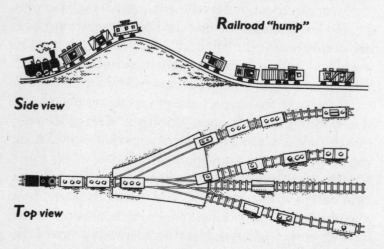

Railroad "hump"

Side view

Top view

by moving cars around one at a time with a switch engine, but that wastes time.

Long ago somebody had the bright idea of building a hill in the middle of the freight yard called a "hump." A single track runs up one side of the hill, and on the way down the other side it branches into many tracks. (See illustration.)

The railroad workers push a string of freight cars to the top of the hill, then give them a shove one at a time down the other side. A worker in a nearby switch tower pulls levers or pushes buttons to line up the rails so each car rolls onto the right track.

Getting the cars to start rolling down the hill may be easy, but getting them to stop at the bottom is something else.

Special steel devices on the rails called "retarders" are supposed to rub on the wheels of passing freight cars and slow them down. Sometimes these devices work, but sometimes they don't. If they don't, the car stops the hard way—by crashing into the car in front of it.

That's bad enough with an ordinary freight car. But if it's a tank car filled with dangerous chemicals, it could be disastrous. If the tank car sprang a leak, the chemicals could escape and in no time the whole neighborhood would smell like Clorox.

To avoid this, many tank cars have DO NOT HUMP stenciled on their sides. (You might also see a DO NOT HUMP sign stuck on the door of a boxcar that contained glassware or something else easily breakable.) This tells the railroad workers to set the car aside for special handling.

Of course, railroad workers being what they are (I used to work on a railroad), they might still smash the tank car into the one in front of it with the switch engine during "special handling." But all you can do is try.

How come the hot water comes blasting out when you first turn it on, but within a few minutes it slows to a trickle?

Things expand when they get warm, right? (Well, they do. Take my word for it.) In most water faucets there's a rubber washer that's supposed to keep the faucet from dripping when the water is turned off. When you turn the water on, this washer is lifted up to allow the water to flow through.

If the water is hot, it can cause the washer to expand after a while. This chokes off the flow of water. The solution? Get a new washer. Or else just open the tap more. You could have worse problems.

Is it true that hot water freezes faster than cold water?

This is one of those old stories you usually hear from somebody's grandmother. Most of these stories are baloney—but not this one.

Let's get one thing straight first. If you've got ordinary cold water (say, 40 degrees Fahrenheit) and ordinary hot water (125 degrees, for example, the hottest you usually can get out of the faucet), the cold water will freeze faster than the hot water.

On the other hand, if you've got very hot water (165 degrees) and very, *very* hot water (195 degrees, or just a little below the boiling point, 212 degrees), the 195 degree water will freeze faster than the 165 degree stuff.

How can this be? There are a couple of things at work. The first is evaporation. Water evaporates more quickly at high temperatures. When it's near the boiling point, it's evaporating *very* quickly, so much so that after a while there isn't that much water left. The less water you've got, the less heat it can hold, and the faster it freezes.

Another thing about evaporation: The water that evaporates carries a lot of heat away with it. (That's the whole idea behind evaporation, remember? The hottest, fastest molecules escape from the water into the air, leaving the slower, cooler molecules behind.) The more evaporation you have, the cooler the remaining water gets, and the faster it will freeze.

There are a couple of other things involved, too, but no need to strain ourselves. Remember, it's not that hot water freezes faster than cold, it's that *very* hot water freezes faster than merely hot. Gotta be careful about these fine points.

WHY DOES THE DRAIN PIPE ON A SINK ALWAYS HAVE THAT FUNNY BEND IN IT?

Maybe you've never noticed this. Maybe, in fact, you have no idea what I'm talking about. Well, I've spent a lot

P-trap

of time crawling around underneath sinks (don't ask), and I know about these things. Allow me to provide the helpful illustration shown above.

Every properly installed drain pipe has a little jog in it called a **P-trap,** because it looks like a *P* on its side. You might think the P-trap is there to catch dirt, but it's not.

Drains empty into sewers or septic tanks. As the stuff in those sewers or tanks decays, it gives off a smelly, explo-

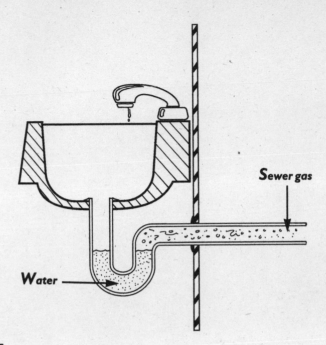

The water in the P-trap prevents sewer gas from backing up into your house.

sive gas—something you definitely want to keep out of your house.

That's what the P-trap is for. When you empty the sink, water flows through the P-trap and out into the sewer. But a small amount stays behind in the trap. The water then keeps the sewer gas from backing up into your house. (See illustration.)

Of course, if the P-trap clogs, you have to take it apart or call a plumber. But it's a small price to pay for not having your house smell like a sewer.

INDEX

ABOUT THE AUTHOR

Ed Zotti is the editor of "The Straight Dope," a syndicated column appearing in alternative newspapers throughout the United States. He has also edited two collections of columns, *The Straight Dope* and *More of the Straight Dope*. A third collection, *Return of the Straight Dope*, is scheduled for publication in 1994. A graduate of Northwestern's Medill School of Journalism, Zotti lives in Chicago with his wife Mary and two children, Ryan and Annie.